Radar Fundamentals

PRENTICE-HALL SERIES IN ELECTRONIC TECHNOLOGY
IRVING L. KOSOW, EDITOR
CHARLES M. THOMSON, JOSEPH J. GERSHON,
AND JOSEPH A. LABOK, CONSULTING EDITORS

ANDERSON, SANTANELLI AND KULIS *Direct Current Circuits and Measurements: A Self-Instructional Programed Manual*

ANDERSON, SANTANELLI AND KULIS *Alternating Current Circuits and Measurements: A Self-Instructional Programed Manual*

BABB *Pulse Circuits: Switching and Shaping*

BARRINGTON *High Vacuum Engineering*

BENEDICT AND WEINER *Industrial Electronic Circuits and Applications*

BRANSON *Introduction to Electronics*

DOYLE *Pulse Fundamentals*

FEDERAL ELECTRIC CORPORATION *Mathematics for Electronics: A Self-Instructional Programed Manual*

FEDERAL ELECTRIC CORPORATION *Special Purpose Transistors: A Self-Instructional Programed Manual*

FEDERAL ELECTRIC CORPORATION *Transistors: A Self-Instructional Programed Manual*

FLORES *The Digital Computer*

HEWLETT-PACKARD *Microwave Theory and Measurements*

JACKSON *Introduction to Electric Circuits, 2nd Ed.*

JOHNSON *Servomechanisms*

KOSOW *Electric Machinery and Control*

LITTON INDUSTRIES *Digital Computer Fundamentals*

MANDL *Directory of Electronic Circuits with a Glossary of Terms*

MANDL *Fundamentals of Electric and Electronic Circuits*

MANDL *Fundamentals of Electronic Computers: Digital and Analog*

MARTIN *Technical Television*

O'NEAL *Electronic Data Processing Systems: A Self-Instructional Programed Manual*

PHILCO TECHNOLOGICAL CENTER *Electronic Precision Measurement Techniques and Experiments*

PHILCO TECHNOLOGICAL CENTER *Servomechanism Fundamentals and Experiments*

POLLACK *Applied Physics*

PRENSKY *Electronic Instrumentation*

RCA INSTITUTES *Basic Electronics: Autotext—A Programed Course*

RCA SERVICE COMPANY *Fundamentals of Transistors: A Programed Text*

RASKHODOFF *Electronic Drafting and Design*

SHIERS *Design and Construction of Electronic Equipment*

SHIERS *Electronic Drafting*

WHEELER *Introduction to Microwaves*

WHEELER *Radar Fundamentals*

Radar Fundamentals

GERSHON J. WHEELER

Manager, Advanced Systems Technology Dept.
Sylvania Electronic Systems — West

PRENTICE-HALL, INC. / ENGLEWOOD CLIFFS, NEW JERSEY

PRENTICE-HALL INTERNATIONAL, INC., *London*
PRENTICE-HALL OF AUSTRALIA, PTY. LTD., *Sydney*
PRENTICE-HALL OF CANADA, LTD., *Toronto*
PRENTICE-HALL OF INDIA PRIVATE LTD., *New Delhi*
PRENTICE-HALL OF JAPAN, INC., *Tokyo*

CURRENT PRINTING (LAST DIGIT): 10 9 8 7 6 5 4 3 2 1

Preface

This book presents a nontechnical explanation of what radar is and how it works. A chapter is devoted to each major subsystem of the radar system (e.g., receiver, transmitter, antenna), describing what the subsystem does and how it works. Different radar systems are explained in terms of these building blocks. Included also are step-by-step explanations of the thinking processes involved in designing a system for a specific application, in testing a radar system, and in designing space applications.

The book was specifically written as a textbook for a one-semester course in radar at the technical institute or junior college level, and as a supplementary text in any course in radio communications or electronics. It should also be useful to the engineer or layman desiring a simple understanding of the subject.

I would like to acknowledge the assistance of Morton Lipman, who read and criticized the text and prepared the problems at the end of each chapter. Special thanks, also, are due Miss Shirley Jackson for typing and proofreading the manuscript.

GERSHON J. WHEELER

Contents

3   MEASURABLE TARGET CHARACTERISTICS   25

4   C-W RADAR   36

5   PULSED-DOPPLER RADAR   48

Key to Symbols

A	area	P_B	power of beacon transmitter
A_B	effective area of beacon antenna	P_H	power in horizontal component
A_e	effective area	P_p	peak power
B	bandwidth	P_R	received power
BW	beamwidth (also θ)	P_T	transmitted power
c	speed of light	P_V	power in vertical component
C.R.	compression ratio	p.r.f.	pulse repetition frequency
D	diameter or aperture width		(also f_r)
d	distance	R	range
E	voltage vector	$R_{\max}$	maximum range
F	focus of parabola	R_R	range from receiver to target
F	noise factor	R_T	range from transmitter to target
F_{db}	noise figure	S_B	minimum detectable signal of
F_T	overall noise factor		beacon receiver
f_b	beat frequency	S_{db}	sensitivity
f_d	Doppler frequency	S_i	input signal
f_r	pulse repetition frequency (also p.r.f.)	$S_{\min}$	minimum detectable signal
		S/N	signal-to-noise ratio
f_t	transmitted frequency	S_o	output signal
G	gain	T	temperature
G_B	gain of beacon antenna	t_r	rise time of pulse
G_R	gain of receiving antenna	v	velocity of target
G_T	gain of transmitting antenna	v_r	radial velocity
h	height	α	attenuation
K	Boltzmann's constant	η	efficiency of illumination
L	loss factor	θ	beamwidth (also BW)
M	moisture	λ	free-space wavelength
N	noise	σ	angular error
n	an integer, number of pulses	σ	radar cross section
N_i	input noise	σ_B	bistatic radar cross section
N_o	output noise	τ	pulse width
N.P.	noise power	ω_s	scan rate
P_A	average power		

Radar Fundamentals

CHAPTER ONE

The Parts of a Radar System

1-1 THE BASIC SYSTEM

The word *radar* is derived from the expression *radio detection and ranging*. Thus, as it was originally conceived, radio waves were utilized to detect the presence of a target and to determine its distance or range. In simplest form, a radio transmitter emits electromagnetic radiation. When the radio wave is interrupted by any object such as a plane, ship, or even a mountain or other land mass, part of the energy is reflected back to a radio receiver located near the transmitter. The reflection is called an *echo*, and the object reflecting it is called a *target*. The presence of an echo indicates that a target has been detected. If the target is one that was sought, the echo is referred to as a *target signal* or simply a *signal*. If, however, echoes are reflected from unwanted targets which make it difficult to select the desired target, the unwanted echoes are called *clutter*.

The time duration from the transmission of the original energy to the reception of the echo is a measure of the range or distance of the target. The velocity of electromagnetic waves in free space is approximately 1000 ft per microsecond. Therefore, if an object is one nautical mile away (6080 ft), it will take slightly more than 12 μsec (microseconds) for the transmitted energy to reach the target and return.

If the transmitter were running continuously, echoes from a target would be detected continuously, and it would be difficult to determine which part of the echo was associated with a particular part of the transmitted energy. Therefore, a common practice is to *pulse-modulate* the transmitter. That is, the RF energy is emitted in short, high-power pulses. The echoes return in short pulses also, and since during reception the transmitter is off, it is possible to associate a given echo with a specific transmitted pulse, and so determine

1

range. Radar using pulse modulation, referred to as pulse radar, is the most common type. However, there are other methods of associating the echoes with the transmissions, and these will be discussed later.

Since, in a pulse radar, the transmitter and receiver are not in use simultaneously, one antenna system can be used for both. The antenna is connected to the transmitter during the short transmission pulse and is then switched to the receiver to detect echoes. It is switched back to the transmitter when the next pulse is emitted.

The basic system is illustrated in Fig. 1-1. The *control circuit* synchronizes the transmitter and receiver and furnishes a time base for the indicator so that time differences can be measured. The *indicator* is usually some form of visual display which enables the operator to determine the presence of a reflected signal and to measure time intervals and, therefore, distances. All a-c and d-c voltages for the circuits are furnished by the *power supply*.

A radar system (or simply, a radar) has many parts or subsystems. This is analogous to the "human" system which has, as subsystems, a nervous system, an arterial system, a digestive system, etc. Similarly, the radar system has subsystems such as the receiving system, the control system, and the transmitter system. The word system is frequently omitted in referring to the whole radar or any of its components.

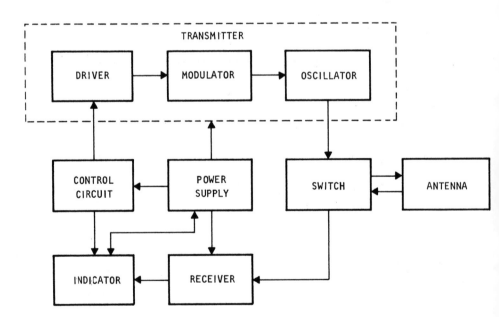

Fig. 1-1. Basic radar circuit.

1-2 PULSE CONSIDERATIONS

The electromagnetic energy transmitted from a pulse radar is emitted in the form of short bursts of energy called pulses. The *pulse repetition frequency* (p.r.f.) is the number of pulses emitted per second. It is desirable to have an echo of a pulse return to the radar before the next pulse is emitted, in order to avoid ambiguities. For example, if the pulses are 500 μsec apart and echoes are received 100 μsec after each pulse, the echoes may be caused by a target 100 μsec away or 600 μsec away. (Assuming about 12 μsec per mile, this would mean about 8 miles or 50 miles.) To avoid this ambiguity, we choose the repetition frequency so that all detectable targets will appear before the next pulse is emitted. In the foregoing example, if it is known that no targets exist beyond 30 miles, for example, then a pulse interval of 500 μsec is permissible. If, on the other hand, the radar is looking for targets as far as 50 miles away, then the pulse interval must be greater than 600 μsec. Note that the *pulse interval* is the reciprocal of the pulse repetition frequency. That is,

$$\text{pulse interval} = \frac{1}{\text{p.r.f.}} \tag{1-1}$$

Thus a pulse interval of 500 μsec corresponds to a repetition frequency of 2000; $(500 \times 10^{-6} = \frac{1}{2000})$. The interval necessary to avoid ambiguities fixes the maximum repetition frequency.

In typical radars, the antenna moves constantly in search of echoes. As the RF beam passes a target, echoes will reflect from the target only as long as pulses hit the target. Since a certain minimum number of echoes is necessary to produce an indication at the receiver, then the number of pulses hitting the target during each pass of the antenna must exceed this minimum. The minimum p.r.f., then, is fixed by the antenna speed and by the receiver and indicator requirements.

The width of the pulse is determined by the minimum range. That is, the transmitter must be turned off and the antenna switched to the receiver by the time the echo from the nearest target of interest comes back. Thus, if the pulse width is 1 μsec, anything closer than $\frac{1}{12}$ mile would not be seen. On the other hand, the pulses cannot be too short, or the amount of energy being reflected will be insufficient to be detected by the receiver. The pulse width also determines the minimum separation of two targets which can be distinguished by the radar. This will be discussed in detail in Sec. 3-4.

1-3 DUTY CYCLE

A typical pulse envelope is shown in Fig. 1-2. The pulse repetition frequency is designated f_r, and $1/f_r$ is the pulse interval. The pulse width is τ.

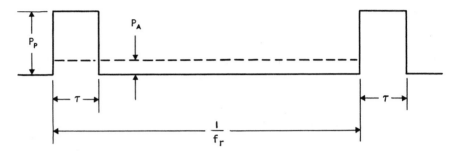

Fig. 1-2. Pulse envelope.

The power emitted during the pulse is called the *peak power*, and it is designated P_p. If the transmitter were running continuously, putting out the same total amount of energy, it would emit a much lower power level, indicated as P_A in the figure. This is called the *average power*. The peak power P_p is on for a duration τ, and this is equivalent (in total energy) to a continuous average power P_A on for a duration $1/f_r$. Thus,

$$P_p \times \tau = P_A \times \frac{1}{f_r}$$

or
$$P_A = P_p \times \tau f_r \qquad (1\text{-}2)$$

The product of pulse width times repetition frequency, τf_r, is called the *duty cycle*. Thus, if a pulse lasts 1 μsec and is repeated 800 times a second, then

$$\text{duty cycle} = 1 \times 10^{-6} \times 800 = 0.0008 \quad \text{or} \quad 0.08 \text{ percent}$$

The average power, as indicated in Eq. 1-2, is equal to the product of the peak power times the duty cycle. In the case just discussed, the average power is 0.08 percent of the peak power.

1-4 THE TIMER

The control circuit is frequently called the *timer* or *timing circuit*, since its chief function is to furnish a time signal which synchronizes the transmitter and the indicator. In some radars there is no separate timing circuit, but instead, the transmitter generates its own pulses which synchronize the indicator and the modulator. However, where it is important to control the pulse width or repetition frequency accurately, it is preferable to have a separate control circuit. The timing circuit is then made up of an oscillator and some pulse-shaping circuits. The oscillator may generate a sine-wave signal or a string of rectangular or irregular pulses. The output of the oscillator is then shaped, usually by differentiating and clipping circuits, to form the type of impulse which will trigger the transmitter and the indicator. The control circuit also furnishes *marking pulses* for the indicator. These are pips or other markings on the face of the indicator which are accurately spaced in time from the inception of the pulse. These markers can then be used to determine the range of a target when the echo appears on the indicator.

1-5 THE TRANSMITTER

As mentioned earlier, the transmitter of a radar may be self-pulsed, in effect functioning as both a transmitter and a timer. This type of transmitter oscillates at both an audio frequency (the pulse repetition rate) and a radio frequency (the carrier). A small portion of the audio frequency is then tapped off to control the indicator.

In most radars, the transmitter receives its timing pulses from a control circuit. The transmitter is then simply a high-power RF oscillator modulated by a pulse modulator which, in effect, turns the transmitter on (during a pulse) and off (during the inter-pulse interval). If the relatively weak signal generated by the timing circuit is insufficient to trigger the modulator, the transmitter will also contain a trigger amplifier, or driver, as shown in Fig. 1-1.

1-6 THE CARRIER FREQUENCY

The choice of frequency is determined by the types of oscillators available, power and range considerations, directivity desired, and atmospheric and propagation effects. The higher the frequency, the shorter the wavelength. Thus, a given antenna size is effectively "larger" at higher frequencies because its aperture is more wavelengths long. This makes a more directive beam. On the other hand, higher-power tubes are available at lower frequencies. Again, higher frequencies are attenuated more in propagation, but if the frequency is too low, the antenna size required is impractical. Radars have been operated successfully from 100 megacycles per second (MHz) to light frequencies of millions of millions of cycles per second (Hz). Most radars operate between 1000 and 20 000 MHz. During World War II, radar frequencies were given letter designations which have stuck. The frequencies near 10 000 MHz are called X-band, those near 3000 are S-band, and those near 1000 are called L-band. The exact frequency limits of the designated bands are not well-delineated. Thus, 2000 MHz is sometimes S and sometimes L. Other less frequently used designations are C-band for frequencies around 5000 MHz, K_u for 18 000, K for 25 000, and K_a for 35 000 MHz.

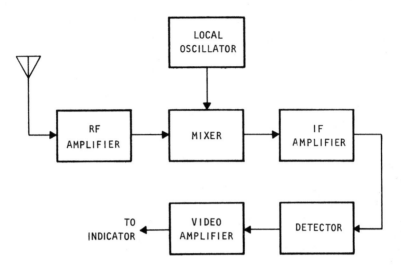

Fig. 1-3. Superheterodyne receiver.

1-7 THE RECEIVER

There are two basic types of radar receivers, the superheterodyne and the video receiver. The superheterodyne receiver is shown in block diagram in Fig. 1-3. The signal from the antenna is fed to one or more RF amplifiers if an improved noise figure is required. If not, the RF amplifier may be omitted and the signal fed right to the mixer. A local oscillator (l. o.) running continuously also feeds a signal to the mixer. The l. o. signal beats with the pulsed echoes, and the difference frequency is amplified and detected (or demodulated) to produce a video signal which is fed to the indicator.

In a video receiver, there are no mixer, local oscillator, and RF amplifier. The RF amplifier output is fed directly to a detector and video amplifier. The "superhet" is a more sensitive receiver but also more complicated.

The radar receiver usually is not in a single box which can be identified separately as a receiver. Thus, the RF amplifier is placed close to the antenna, whereas the video amplifier is sometimes inside the indicator case. The other components or circuits are distributed at convenient points in between.

1-8 INDICATORS

The indicator in a radar system is usually a cathode ray oscilloscope and is generally referred to simply as a *scope*. There are many different types of presentations. The simplest is called an *A-scope* and is shown in Fig. 1-4. The horizontal sweep is calibrated in time or range from left to right, and the vertical displacement is simply the amplitude of the signal. The sweep begins with an indication of the transmitted pulse caused by some of the transmitted signal leaking into the receiver deliberately. Any echoes then appear as pips, horizontally displaced. The range of the target can be determined directly from the calibration of the horizontal sweep. In Fig. 1-4, two echoes are shown, one at a range r_1 and a weaker one at a range r_2. It should be noted that the horizontal sweep is not a sharp line; it is a constantly shifting pattern of short vertical lines. This is caused by noise in the receiver and is called *grass*. It will be explained further in the chapter on reception (Chap. 7).

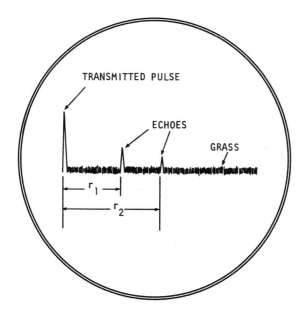

Fig. 1-4. *A*-scope presentation.

The highly directive antenna used with a radar illuminates the target and receives an echo only when it is pointing in the right direction. Thus, when a target appears on the *A*-scope, the operator knows that it is in the same direction that the antenna is pointing. It is also possible to plot range vs. azimuth on the face of the scope. This is called a *B-scope* presentation. Another type, called *C-scope* presentation, plots elevation vertically and azimuth horizontally. The *B*- and *C*-scopes are used infrequently.

The Planned Position Indicator, or PPI presentation, shown in Fig. 1-5, plots a map of the area being scanned. The position of the antenna is represented in Fig. 1-5 by a dot at the center of the scope. A target's *range* is indicated by its distance from the center, which is scaled in time. The target echo (*T* in the figure) appears only when the antenna is pointing at the target, and the bearing angle is indicated by its angular distance from the vertical.

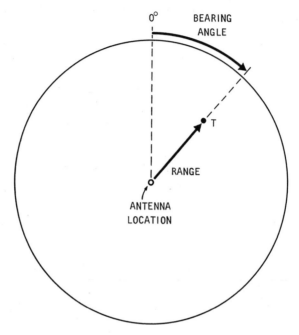

Fig. 1-5. PPI presentation.

PROBLEMS

1-1. What is the difference between pulse width and pulse interval?

1-2. What is the minimum pulse interval of a radar with a fixed antenna which is to detect targets unambiguously at a range of 100 miles? What is the p.r.f. of this radar?   *ans:* 1.2×10^{-3} sec, 833 pps

1-3. Construct a graph of maximum pulse repetition frequency (y-axis) versus unambiguous range (x-axis). Let the x-axis have units of miles, and let it include all ranges between 1 mile and 1000 miles. Use log-log paper. What is the shape of the curve on this type of paper?

1-4. What is the difference between the pulse repetition frequency and the carrier frequency?

1-5. What is the maximum allowable pulse width if we desire to detect targets at a range of one-half mile?

1-6. A radar control circuit is required to produce marking pulses spaced one mile apart. At what frequency should the marking pulse oscillator operate?
                                        ans: 83 kilocycles per second (kHz)

1-7. Let τ be the pulse width and T be the pulse interval. Express the duty cycle in terms of these two quantities.

1-8. A radar has a pulse width of 2 μsec and a p.r.f. of 8000 pps. Target echoes are received 30 μsec and 60 μsec after the transmission of a pulse. Draw an A-scope display with the x-axis in units of miles showing minimum range, maximum unambiguous range, and the two targets. Assume that the closest target has half the amplitude of the more distant target.

1-9. Repeat Prob. 1-8 for a PPI display. Assume that the closest target is due north of the radar and the other target is due east. What is the shape of lines which indicate minimum range and maximum unambiguous range?

1-10. A radar has a pulse width of 2.4 μsec and a maximum unambiguous range of 20 miles. Its average power is 10 watts. What is the peak power?

ans: 1000 watts

1-11. A radar has a pulse width of 4 μsec and a pulse interval of 240 μsec. Can this radar detect targets and unambiguously measure their range if they are located (a) one-half mile from radar? (b) 25 miles from radar? Explain your answer in both cases.

1-12. A radar with a rotating antenna illuminates a target for 0.1 seconds. One hundred received pulses are required for an indication at the receiver. It is also desired that target range be measured unambiguously out to 20 miles. What are the smallest and largest values which the p.r.f. may assume? Can the p.r.f. be 2000 pps?

ans: 1000, 4000 pps

CHAPTER TWO

Antennas

2-1 ANTENNA PURPOSE

A radar antenna may be thought of as a coupling device or transducer between free space and the transmission line from the duplexer. During transmission, energy from the transmitter is switched to the antenna by the duplexer, and the antenna causes the energy to radiate into free space. On reception, a signal in free space impinges on the antenna and is coupled to the transmission line running to thè duplexer, where it is switched to the receiver. By reciprocity, the coupling to free space during transmission is identical with the coupling to the transmission line during reception. Thus, an antenna which has a large effective aperture on reception also has high gain on transmission.

The main function of the antenna is to shape the transmitted beam so that the radiated energy is concentrated in the desired direction in space. In general, a large aperture results in a narrow beamwidth. The narrow beamwidth indicates that the energy is concentrated in one direction, that is, that the antenna has high gain in that direction. On reception, the large aperture intercepts more energy. By reciprocity, the transmission gain is the same as the reception gain.

2-2 GAIN

An antenna which radiates in all directions equally is called an *isotropic radiator* or *source*. There is no such antenna, because every antenna exhibits some directive properties. However, the isotropic antenna is a convenient reference point, and thus the gain or directivity of a given real antenna is expressed as the increase in power radiated in a given direction compared to the power radiated by the fictitious isotropic antenna, assuming the same total power in both cases. If an antenna has directivity, the gain is a function of direction from the antenna. Thus, variation in gain with direction is called the *gain function* of the antenna. The maximum value of the gain function is referred to simply as the *gain* and is designated G. It is measured in decibels (db). A matched transmitting antenna with a gain of 12 db would put out a signal (in the direction in which the signal is maximum) 12 db greater than a signal from an isotropic source which is fed by the same transmitter.

When an antenna is used for receiving, and a plane wave impinges on it, the amount of power intercepted is proportional to its area. However, all points on the antenna do not couple uniformly to the transmission line, so that the amount of energy reaching the receiver is reduced. The *effective area* of the antenna is the area of cross section which, when uniformly coupled to the transmission line, delivers the same energy as the actual antenna. The effective area is thus less than the actual area. The ratio of the two is called the *efficiency of illumination*, and this relationship is expressed as

$$A_e = \eta A \tag{2-1}$$

where η is the efficiency of illumination

   A_e is the effective area

   A is the physical area

The gain of the antenna is proportional to the effective area, as expressed by

$$G = \frac{4\pi A_e}{\lambda^2} = \frac{4\pi \eta A}{\lambda^2} \tag{2-2}$$

where G is the gain

   λ is the free-space wavelength

Equation 2-2 indicates that, for a given antenna, the smaller the wavelength the higher the gain. Thus, at microwaves it is possible to achieve extremely high-gain antennas with realizable physical structures.

2-3 POLARIZATION

All electromagnetic waves consist of an electric (or voltage) field and a magnetic field. These are always perpendicular to each other. By definition, the *polarization* of an electromagnetic wave is the direction of the electric field. If this field is perpendicular to the earth, the wave is vertically polarized; if the voltage field is horizontal, the polarization is horizontal. A field may be at some intermediate angle between 0° and 90°, in which case the field is usually said to have both horizontal and vertical components; it would be just as correct to say that the field is at a specified angle from the vertical or horizontal. Figure 2-1 illustrates a voltage vector which is polarized at an angle θ from the vertical. From the diagram, it is obvious that the vertical component is $E \cos \theta$, and the horizontal component is $E \sin \theta$, where E is the amplitude of the voltage vector of the original wave. The power in the horizontal polarization is the square of the voltage or

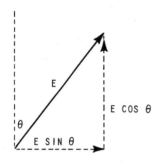

$$P_H = E^2 \sin^2 \theta \qquad (2\text{-}3)$$

Similarly, the power in the vertical polarization is

$$P_V = E^2 \cos^2 \theta \qquad (2\text{-}4)$$

The sum of these two is

Fig. 2-1. Polarization components.

$$P_H + P_V = E^2 (\cos^2 \theta + \sin^2 \theta) = E^2 \qquad (2\text{-}5)$$

which is, of course, the power in the original wave. Thus, a wave polarized at an acute angle to the vertical may be considered equivalent to two component waves traveling together, one horizontally and the other vertically polarized. The antenna determines the polarization of the radiated field. If an antenna launches a horizontally polarized wave, the antenna is said to be horizontally polarized.

A horizontally polarized antenna launches a wave which has no vertical components. By reciprocity then, such an antenna will receive no vertical components. Thus, for maximum efficiency, the transmitting and receiving antennas should have the same polarization. If the receiving antenna is polarized at 90° with respect to the transmitting antenna, it will receive no signal. Such antennas are said to be *cross polarized*. Maximum reception occurs when the antennas have the same polarization, minimum when they are cross polarized. In between, the amplitude varies as the cosine of the angle between the two antennas.

Sometimes it is necessary to transmit signals to a point where the polarization of the receiving antenna is unknown and may be at any angle. A common solution is to transmit *circularly polarized* waves. In circular polarization, the polarization of the wave rotates at the RF rate. At any moment in time, the voltage vector has a component correctly oriented for the receiving antenna and one perpendicular to this. Thus, half the power will be received, regardless of the polarization of the receiving antenna. Similarly, when searching for signals of random polarization, a circularly polarized antenna can be used on reception.

An antenna which has a single direction of polarization (as opposed to circular) is said to be *plane polarized*. Such an antenna can be used to determine the polarization of a transmitted signal simply by rotating it until the received signal is maximum. If the amplitude of the received signal stays constant as the plane-polarized receiving antenna is rotated, then the transmitted signal must be circularly polarized. If the amplitude decreases to zero in one polarization and is maximum 90° from this, then the direction of polarization is that at which the amplitude is maximum. Sometimes the signal has no zero polarization and is not constant, either. This is *elliptical polarization*, which, in general, is not deliberately transmitted, but is imperfect circular polarization.

2-4 BEAM PATTERN

If the waveguide[1] is left open, a wave propagating in the guide will radiate from the open end. Since the waveguide impedance differs from that of free space, not all the energy will be radiated, but some will be reflected back toward the generator. A simple matching iris or post can be used to match the open waveguide so that all the power is in fact radiated. The open guide is therefore an antenna, but from Eq. (2-2), it is evidently a low-gain antenna. Thus, if the waveguide is 0.4 in. $\times$ 0.9 in. (*X*-band), *A* is 0.36 in.[2] At 10 000 MHz, λ is 1.18 in. From Eq. (2-2),

$$G = \frac{4\pi(0.36)}{1.39} = 3.25 \approx 5 \text{ db}$$

Equation (2-2) assumes a uniform distribution across the waveguide aperture so that the effective area is the actual area. As a matter of fact, it is obvious that the aperture distribution is not uniform. The voltage is maximum at the center of the waveguide and is zero at the side walls. The same distribution is carried to the aperture. The result of such nonuniform distribution is to produce an effective area which is less than the 0.36 in.[2] indicated. Consequently, the gain also will be less than the 5 db mentioned before.

Equation (2-2) indicates that the larger the effective area, the larger is the gain. Since a larger gain means that more energy is transmitted in a preferred direction, it must of necessity imply that this extra energy is taken from other directions so that the beam of energy becomes narrower. In general, the larger the aperture becomes in terms of wavelengths, the narrower is the beam.

The relative intensity of the radiation as a function of direction can be

---

[1] G. J. Wheeler, *Introduction to Microwaves* (Englewood Cliffs, N. J.: Prentice-Hall, Inc., 1963), pp. 56ff.

plotted in polar coordinates, as shown typically in Fig. 2-2. This is called a *beam pattern*, or simply, a pattern of the antenna. The beam pattern for the *E*-plane is usually different from that in the *H*-plane. This can be easily understood by considering an antenna consisting of a single vertical wire, half a wavelength long. It will radiate equally well in all horizontal directions so that its azimuth pattern is a circle. In elevation, however, it may have zero radiation off the ends and maximum radiation straight ahead. Since the wire is vertical, the voltage field is vertical and the magnetic field is horizontal. Thus, the pattern in the horizontal plane is in the plane of the magnetic field and is called the *H*-plane pattern. Similarly, the elevation pattern is the *E*-plane pattern. Of course, if the wire were horizontal, the azimuth pattern would be the *E*-plane pattern.

The pattern of Fig. 2-2 indicates that there is a favored direction of propagation for the antenna in the indicated plane of polarization (in this case the *E*-plane). The other plane of polarization may be similar or may be entirely different. The largest lobe in the figure is called the *main lobe*; smaller lobes are called *sidelobes*. If there is a lobe 180° from the main lobe, it is called a *back lobe*.

In many types of microwave antennas, a small radiator illuminates a reflector or lens which then redirects the energy into free space. The small primary radiator has a beam pattern of its own which is called the *primary pattern* of the composite antenna. The pattern of the whole antenna is strictly the *secondary pattern*, but it is usually simply the pattern.

The width of the main lobe of the pattern at the half-power points is called the *beamwidth* of the antenna. Just as the *E*- and *H*-planes have different patterns, so also do they have different beamwidths. It should be noted that beam patterns can be plotted in decibels against angular direction (as in Fig. 2-2), in power, or in voltage. The half-power points are the 3-db points on the decibel plot, the 0.5 points on the power plot, or the 0.707 points on the voltage plot. The chart is always normalized so that the maximum point is unity or zero decibels. In Fig. 2-2, the beamwidth is 20°.

2-5 SIDELOBES

To achieve maximum gain from an antenna, the aperture must be illuminated uniformly and in phase by the feed to the antenna. When this happens, the gain of the antenna is a function of the area of the aperture and is given by Eq. (2-2). There is a disadvantage in this arrangement, however, in that the discontinuity presented by the edge of the antenna occurs at a point of high intensity, which produces sidelobes. Sidelobes, of course, are undesirable since they may give erroneous indications of direction. If the

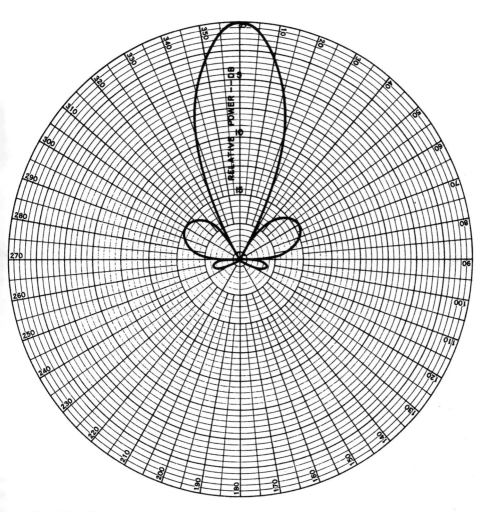

Fig. 2-2. Beam pattern.

discontinuity represented by the antenna edge is at a point of lower intensity, the sidelobes would be reduced. Thus, it is customary to strive for a tapered illumination of the aperture, with maximum intensity at the center, tapering to 10 db down at the edge. This reduces the sidelobes but also reduces the gain, since the tapered radiation from the aperture is equivalent to uniform radiation from a smaller aperture.

For a perfectly symmetrical antenna, the pattern should also be symmetrical. However, mechanical tolerances would be too stringent to accomplish this. In practice, there is always some asymmetry which shows up particularly in unsymmetrical sidelobes.

For a parabolic reflector, uniformly illuminated, the gain is as given by Eq. (2-2), and the sidelobes are down 13 db, that is, the peak of the nearest sidelobes is 13 db below the peak of the main beam. If the parabola is illuminated so that the circumference is 10 db below the center, the sidelobes are reduced to 17 db below the main beam. The gain is also reduced to about 55 percent of the value given in Eq. (2-2). The antenna is then said to have an efficiency of 55 percent. The gain may be further reduced by *aperture blocking*, such as when a part of the feed system is in front of the dish.

2-6 BEAMWIDTH

In Sec. 2-4, beamwidth was defined as the width of the beam at the half-power points. Inasmuch as the gain and sidelobe level of an antenna pattern vary with the aperture illumination, it might be expected that the beamwidth would also vary, and this is indeed the case. In general, the beamwidth is inversely proportional to the aperture width. Also, if the aperture is uniformly illuminated, it is effectively larger than the same aperture with tapered illumination and thus will have a narrower beam.

A parabolic dish antenna with tapered illumination down 10 db at the edges has a beamwidth in degrees given by

$$\text{BW} = \frac{70\lambda}{D} \tag{2-6}$$

where λ is the free-space wavelength, and D is the diameter of the dish. The beamwidth is the same for both E-plane and H-plane patterns, since the same illumination is assumed for both. In practice, it would be difficult to build a feed with a primary pattern which illuminates the dish so that the taper is the same in all directions from the center out so the perimeter of the dish. Thus, the E- and H-plane patterns usually are not the same.

The simple waveguide antenna described in Sec. 2-4 can be matched by flaring the walls of the waveguide gradually until the impedance of the enlarged guide approximates that of free space. Such a horn antenna has a gain which is directly related to the area of the aperture. But since this aperture is not uniformly illuminated, the efficiency is never 100 percent. In practice, the efficiency of a horn antenna is between 50 and 80 percent. The aperture is, of course, a large waveguide in which the voltage is maximum at the center and zero at the side walls. In the H-plane then, the distribution is maximum at the center, tapering to zero at the walls. The H-plane beamwidth is given by Eq. (2-6), just as for a parabola with tapered illumination, but D here is the dimension of the aperture in the H-plane. Since there is no variation in illumination in the E-plane direction, for $TE_{1,0}$ mode[2] excitation, the E-plane beamwidth will be narrower for a given dimension than the H-plane pattern. The E-plane beamwidth in degrees is

$$\text{BW} = \frac{51\lambda}{D} \tag{2-7}$$

where D now is the dimension across the horn in the E-plane. Equation (2-7) is also the beamwidth of a uniformly illuminated parabolic dish.

The *shape* of the beam is a function of the antenna shape. An antenna may be designed with a uniform beamwidth in all planes. This is usually a narrow-beam pattern and is called a *pencil beam*. For some applications, a pattern is required which is narrow in azimuth and very wide in elevation, or vice versa. This *fan beam* is obtained by having an aperture which is wide in the dimension requiring a narrow beam, and narrow in the other direction.

Pencil beams are used where it is required to measure the angular position of a target in both azimuth and elevation. Ordinarily, this type of beam is used after a target is acquired and it is necessary to track the target. The fan beam is more suited to searching for targets. A single fan beam with a narrow beamwidth in azimuth can detect the azimuthal position of any target quickly, but it will yield no elevation information. If the height of the target is known (e.g., in searching for ships), no other beam is necessary to locate the target. However, in searching for planes, two fan beams are sometimes used, one with its narrow beamwidth in azimuth and the other in elevation.

2-7   PARABOLIC ANTENNAS

The paraboloid or parabolic dish is usually used as a reflector in microwave systems because of two special geometric properties. These are illustrated in Fig. 2-3 in a simple parabola. First, all the rays from a fixed point, called the focal point, to the parabola are reflected as parallel rays. The focal point or focus is designated F in Fig. 2-3. Secondly, the sum of the distances from F to the parabola, and then along the reflected ray to some reference plane, PP', is a constant. Thus, the reflected wave is made up of parallel rays which are all in phase.

The simple round dish, the paraboloid, should be fed ideally by a point source at F, the focal point. Furthermore, this point source must have the correct primary pattern to produce the desired tapered illumination of the

---

[2] Cf. Wheeler, *op. cit.*, pp. 58ff.

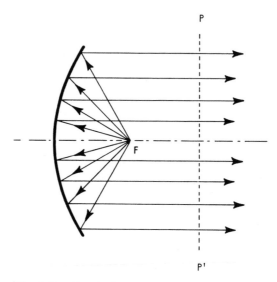

Fig. 2-3.   Parabola.

aperture. In practice, the feed is usually a small horn located at the focal
point, but occasionally a dipole may be used. Power from the transmitter
is brought to the feed by a waveguide or coaxial line passing through a hole
in the center of the dish or passing around the side of the dish. In either case,
the feed line and feed intercept the energy reflected from the parabola, causing
some deterioration in the pattern, such as reduced gain and higher sidelobes.
To avoid this deterioration, it is possible to use an *offset-feed* parabolic
antenna. This is simply a portion of a whole paraboloid and is shown in Fig.
2-4. The paraboloid AC has a focal point F. The feed horn is located at F, but
the portion of the paraboloid from B to C is removed. The offset dish AB may
be circular or may be simply half a dish, depending on the desired pattern.
In any case, rays from F will not return to F, and the pattern will not be
affected by the feed and horn.

2-8 CONICAL SCANNING

When a radar is used to direct guns toward a target, the antenna must
indicate the direction of the target quite accurately. In general, a simple
pencil beam cannot indicate direction with sufficient accuracy, since the difference in reflected signal between "on-target" and a "near-miss" is not usually
great enough to detect. Furthermore, when a target is detected, the operator
must swing the beam back and forth through the target to determine when

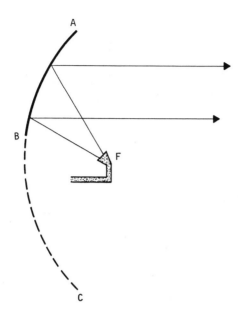

Fig. 2-4. Offset parabola.

the target is at the peak of the beam. In fact, when the target is first detected, it is impossible to tell whether it is on the peak or off to the side; and if off to the side, it is impossible to tell whether the movement should be to the left or to the right.

One method of solving this problem is called *conical scanning*. The beam is made to nutate about an axis as it scans in azimuth or elevation. Thus in a plane through the axis, the beam will occupy extreme positions indicated in Fig. 2-5. At one point in its nutation, it will occupy position *A*, and half a revolution later, position *B*. If a target is in the direction *X* in the figure, the signal received will have an amplitude *a* when the beam is in position *A*, and an amplitude *b* when the beam is at *B*. Thus, the received signal will be modulated at the rate of nutation. If the target is "dead-ahead," on the axis of nutation, there will be *no* modulation, since the amplitude remains the same with nutation. The point where the two extreme positions of the beam cross is called the *crossover point*. It should be from 1 to 3 db below the peak of the beam.

In operation, when a target is detected somewhere near the beam center, the antenna is moved so that the modulation is decreased. When the modulation reaches zero, the axis of nutation is pointing right at the target.

The nutation of the beam is usually accomplished by positioning the feed

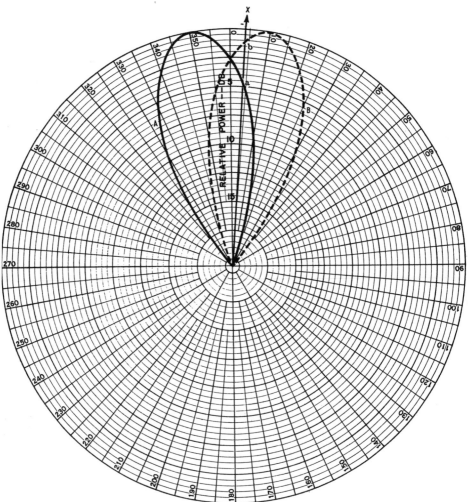

Fig. 2-5. Conical scanning.

horn slightly off the focal point of the parabola and rotating the horn around the focal point. The location of the horn off the focal point produces only a slight degradation in pattern.

2-9 MONOPULSE

If instead of a single nutating antenna, two antennas are used pointing in slightly different directions, the lobes would have a configuration similar to that of Fig. 2-5 for conical scanning. Instead of a modulation, there would now be two received signals. On "boresight," the two signals would have the same amplitudes, but if the target were "off-center," the amplitudes would differ. It is possible to use two feeds and one dish as well as two separate antennas.

Again, the two antennas could be pointed in the same direction, that is, with beams parallel. If the antennas are separated slightly, a signal from a target would arrive at the two antennas at different times, that is, in different phases, unless the target was right on the line midway between the two antennas.

In both cases, the target direction can be determined accurately without the mechanical motion and its associated problems in conical scanning. With proper circuitry, the two signals can be compared automatically in phase or amplitude so that the target will be tracked. Suitable arrangements of two or four antennas can be used to obtain information in both azimuth and elevation.

The systems which use two or more antennas in this way are called *monopulse* or *simultaneous lobing systems.* Their main advantage over conical scanning is they have no moving parts. However, the circuitry is more intricate, and the system is more susceptible to spurious responses.

2-10 SEQUENTIAL LOBING

In conical scanning, the antenna beam nutates continuously around a fixed axis. Figure 2-5 indicated two extreme positions of the beam. Instead of rotating one beam, it should be possible to use two fixed beams which always occupied these same extreme positions. If the beams are alternately connected to a single receiver, the resultant modulation would indicate direction in the plane of the two beams just as in the case of conical scanning. This method is called *sequential lobing.* In practice, it is common to use four feeds, producing four beams at 90° intervals around the axis of "rotation." The beams are switched on (that is, they are connected to the receiver) sequentially, and the modulation indicates the direction of the target. This system has no moving parts, but does require four feeds and suitable switches.

2-11 SCANNING

The word *scanning* is used in two different senses in radar applications. As indicated in Secs. 2-8 through 2-10, scanning is used to track a target which has already been acquired. In this sense, scanning refers to comparing target returns from two or more beam positions in order to determine the angular position of the target accurately. Scanning also refers to searching for targets. The radar beam is made to sweep over a large sector or even over a hemisphere. The whole dish with its feed assembly is moved physically so that the beam points in different directions.

To cover the required volume in space systematically, the antenna is moved according to some prescribed pattern. In *helical scan*, the antenna beam rotates through 360° in azimuth while it is slowly raised in elevation. In the *spiral scan*, the beam rotates in a spiral. The helical scan covers a hemisphere, while the spiral scan is usually limited to a conical volume. Scans for rectangular shapes consist simply of passing the antenna beam across the space, advancing slightly with each pass. The passes may be horizontal or vertical.

In high-powered radars, especially at lower microwave frequencies and u.h.f., the antenna is too large to move. These radars are usually used to detect a threat a great distance away and coming from a known general direction. The large antenna is usually fixed and is made to scan over a limited area by moving its feed off the focal point. The feed can be moved appropriately for any limited type of scan. There is some pattern deterioration, but it can be tolerated.

2-12 PHASED ARRAYS

A phased array is made up of a number of individual antennas suitably spaced and fed so that a fixed beam is produced in a desired direction. By changing the relative phases of the signals at each antenna, the direction of the beam is varied. That is, the beam can be made to scan. The relative phase shift can be changed by varying phase shifters in individual feeds electronically, or by changing frequency so that fixed path lengths vary in terms of wavelengths.

High-powered phased arrays may consist of several individual elements, each one fed from its own amplifier. Thus, it is possible to build a high-powered radar without requiring a tube capable of handling the total power. The beam may be scanned electronically without any physical movement. The antenna elements are usually dipoles or waveguide slots, although any type of radiating structure could be used.

2-13 INTERFEROMETER

An interferometer is a type of phased array in which only a few elements, spaced many wavelengths apart, are used. The pattern is then a series of uniform lobes and deep nulls, similar to the lines produced by an optical interferometer. When a target is detected by an interferometer, it could lie in any lobe, so that its exact angular position is ambiguous. However, as the target moves, the change of angle can be read very accurately. When used in conjunction with other devices which determine approximate angle, the interferometer gives more accurate angular measurements than any other antenna.

It is possible to space the elements randomly, in effect producing more than one interferometer with lobes of different widths. This arrangement can resolve the ambiguities in the measurement of absolute angle.

2-14 DUPLEXERS

A device which permits the use of a single antenna for both transmitting and receiving is called a *duplexer*. This may be a switch, as shown in Fig. 1-1, which connects the antenna to the transmitter during the transmission time and to the receiver during the inter-pulse intervals. Mechanical switches have been used, but they are not reliable and generally cannot switch fast enough. A power-sensitive switch, called a T-R (for transmit-receive), is frequently used. The high peak power in the pulse causes a breakdown in the T-R so that it looks like a short circuit. The T-R is placed in front of the receiver, and in the fired condition, it isolates the receiver from the transmitted power. During reception, low-power signals from the antenna pass through the T-R to the receiver.

In c-w radars, which will be considered later, both the transmitter and receiver must be operating continuously. The duplexer in a c-w system must isolate the transmitter and receiver as well as feed the transmitted signal to the antenna and the received echo from antenna to receiver. This is usually accomplished by using a ferrite circulator as a duplexer.

PROBLEMS

2-1. Express antenna gain in terms of effective area A_e and carrier frequency f.

2-2. The physical area of an antenna is 10 ft², but its effective area is measured to be 7.6 ft². What is the efficiency of illumination of this antenna?   *ans:*   0.76

2-3. A signal is transmitted by an antenna with vertical polarization. In the transmission medium, the signal is reflected from an object and the polarization vector is rotated 180°. Assuming the total received power is 1 watt, how much power would be indicated if the receiving antenna is (a) vertically polarized? (b) horizontally polarized? (c) circularly polarized?

2-4. If the illumination of an antenna is tapered at the edges to reduce sidelobes, what will happen to the gain? What would you expect to happen to the beamwidth?

2-5. An antenna produces a fan beam which has a beamwidth of 20° in the vertical direction and 2° in the horizontal direction. Which antenna dimension is larger, the horizontal dimension or vertical dimension? Give a rough estimate of the ratio of the two dimensions.

2-6. A conical scan antenna is rotated at a rate such that the minimum signal is obtained 0.1 sec. after the maximum signal. At what frequency will the output signal be modulated? *ans:* 5 Hz

2-7. What is the minimum number of pulses required for a sequential lobing system to determine target location? Compare this answer to the minimum number of pulses required for a monopulse system.

2-8. Describe the major difference between an interferometer pattern and a conventional antenna pattern produced by a phased array.

2-9. A parabolic dish antenna which is uniformly illuminated has a beamwidth of 10° and an efficiency of illumination of 100 percent. What is its gain for $\lambda = 1$ ft? Another dish has same beamwidth and illumination for $\lambda = 0.1$ ft. What is its gain? (*Hint:* The area of a circle is $\pi D^2/4$.) *ans:* 129, 129

2-10. Derive a general expression which relates the gain of the antenna of Prob. 2-9 to its beamwidth.

2-11. A horizontally polarized antenna is used to receive a signal whose polarization vector makes a 30° angle with the vertical. What fraction of the signal power is received by the antenna? *ans:* $\frac{1}{4}$

2-12. Two uniformly illuminated, 3-ft diameter, parabolic reflectors are to be used in an amplitude monopulse radar which operates at a frequency of 10 000 MHz. For the 3-db point of each pattern to be located on the boresight, at which angle from the boresight should each beam be tilted? *ans:* 1.67°

2-13. After a certain T-R tube is fired by a 3 μsec pulse, it requires another microsecond before it can pass low-level signals. What is the minimum range of this radar? (*Hint:* See Sec. 1-2.) *ans:* $\frac{1}{3}$ mile

2-14. At what frequency must an antenna with an effective area of 7.9 ft² be excited in order to achieve a gain of 30 db (1000). *ans:* 10 GHz

2-15. What is the major difference between a fan beam and a pencil beam?

CHAPTER THREE

Measurable Target Characteristics

3-1 THE RADAR EQUATION

If a radar transmits a power P_T from an isotropic antenna, at a distance R from the antenna the power will be spread uniformly over an area $4\pi R^2$. Thus the power per unit area is

$$\text{power density} = \frac{P_T}{4\pi R^2} \tag{3-1}$$

Since the radar has an antenna with gain G in a specific direction, the power density is increased in this direction. Thus,

$$\text{power density in direction of maximum signal} = \frac{P_T G}{4\pi R^2} \tag{3-2}$$

At the distance R, a target intercepts the signal and reflects a portion σ of it. Then

$$\text{power reradiated from target} = \frac{P_T G \sigma}{4\pi R^2} \tag{3-3}$$

Back at the radar, the power density of the reradiated signal is the reradiated power divided by the same spherical area. Thus,

$$\text{power density of echo signal at receiving antenna} = \frac{P_T G \sigma}{(4\pi R^2)^2} \tag{3-4}$$

The receiving antenna has an effective area A_e, which captures a received power P_R. Then

$$P_R = \frac{P_T G \sigma A_e}{(4\pi R^2)^2} \tag{3-5}$$

From Eq. (2-2)

$$G = \frac{4\pi A_e}{\lambda^2} \tag{2-2}$$

Thus,

$$P_R = \frac{P_T A_e^2 \sigma}{4\pi \lambda^2 R^4} \tag{3-6}$$

Solving Eq. (3-6) for R,

$$R = \left[\frac{P_T A_e^2 \sigma}{4\pi \lambda^2 P_R}\right]^{1/4} \tag{3-7}$$

If the value of P_R is the minimum detectable signal $S_{\min}$ of the receiver, then

$$R_{\max} = \left[\frac{P_T A_e^2 \sigma}{4\pi \lambda^2 S_{\min}}\right]^{1/4} \tag{3-8}$$

Eq. (3-8) is called the *radar equation*.

From Eq. (3-8), the range R varies as the fourth root of the transmitted power. That is, other things being equal, it is necessary to multiply the transmitted power by 16 in order to double the range. However, it is only necessary to multiply the antenna area by 4 to accomplish the same thing. Increasing the frequency (reducing λ) is another way to increase range.

3-2 RADAR CROSS SECTION

The quantity σ, introduced in Eq. (3-3), is called the *radar cross section* of the target. This is equivalent to an area which would intercept the transmitted signal and reflect isotropically an amount which produces the returned echo. The actual area of the target is usually greater than σ, because some power is absorbed. In fact, in designing countermeasures against radar, one consideration is the use of absorbent materials to reduce the radar cross section. However, in special cases, a target may be designed to have a radar cross section larger than its physical area.

The radar cross section of a target is not constant with frequency. In general, there are three ranges of interest. In the first, the target dimensions are small compared to the wavelength. This is called the *Rayleigh region* after Lord Rayleigh who first studied scattering from small objects (Rayleigh scattering). At the next region, the target dimensions are approximately equal to the wavelength. This is called the *resonance region*. The third region, the *optical region*, is that in which the target dimensions are much greater than the wavelength.

A perfectly conducting sphere of radius r should have a physical cross section of πr^2. At frequencies at which the circumference $(2\pi r)$ is about a wavelength, however, the sphere acts as a resonant element and appears more than three times as big as its true cross section. This is the beginning of the resonant region. As the frequency increases, the radar cross section oscillates about the true cross section, with decreasing amplitude. When the circumference is about ten wavelengths, or more, the radar cross section is the true cross section of the sphere. This is the optical region. At frequencies below resonance (higher wavelength), the sphere appears much smaller. The cross section in the Rayleigh region varies as $1/\lambda^4$. When the circumference is about $\lambda/4$, the sphere appears only about $\frac{1}{30}$ of its true cross section.

These scattering principles are important when it is necessary to choose a frequency to pick out or see through a specific target. For example, if it is desired to detect planes flying during rain storms, a frequency should be chosen so that the rain drops are very small compared to a wavelength. On the other hand, for weather radars it is important to get strong reflections from rain. Here the frequency should be chosen so that the dimensions of the drops lie in the resonant region.

3-3 POLARIZATION

If a thin vertical wire, half a wavelength long, intercepts a vertically polarized signal, it will act as a resonant dipole and reflect a strong signal. In effect, it has a large radar cross section. However, if the transmitted signal is horizontally polarized, the same vertical wire will be virtually invisible. Thus, the radar cross section is dependent on polarization.

A complex target such as a plane or ship has many surfaces and lines which yield individual reflections. The composite of these reflections is dependent on polarization and also on the direction from which the transmitted wave arrives at the target. Experimental measurements of radar cross section of a man range from $\frac{1}{10}$ meter^2 to 2 meters^2 at radar frequencies. The wide spread is the result of different polarizations and aspect angles.

3-4 RANGE

As was mentioned in Chap. 1, range is measured by the time interval between the transmitted pulse and the received echo. Electromagnetic waves travel at the speed of light, which is

$$300 \text{ meters per microsecond} \quad \text{or} \quad 984 \text{ ft per microsecond} \qquad (3\text{-}9)$$

Radar range is usually measured in nautical miles (1 n.mi. = 6080 ft). Thus, the time for a signal to travel to a target 1 n.mi. away and return is

$$t = \frac{12\ 160 \text{ ft}}{984 \text{ ft}/\mu\text{sec}} = 12.4 \ \mu\text{sec}$$

If two targets are in the same direction but at different distances, two separate echoes will be received. They will arrive at different times, and each arrival will indicate the range of a specific target. However, in order to separate the two returns, it is necessary that the second echo arrive after the first one is ended. A wide transmitted pulse will produce a wide return pulse. Hence, the narrower the transmitted pulse, the closer together the two targets can be and still be resolved. The smallest distance which can be discriminated is called the *range resolution* of the radar. Targets which are closer together than this minimum distance appear as one large target.

3-5 ANGLE

The direction of a target is usually specified in terms of two angles, azimuth and elevation. *Azimuth* is the angle in the *horizontal* plane between a fixed reference direction and the direction of the target. The reference direction may be a compass direction such as north, or it may be the direction in which the search radar is moving (for example, on a ship or airplane). The *angle of elevation* is the angle above the horizontal.

As a radar antenna scans, its beam moves across a volume of space. When a target is intercepted, the reflection returns in microseconds, during which time the antenna movement has been infinitesimal. Consequently, when a target signal is detected, it may be assumed to lie in the direction in which the antenna is pointing. Measuring the *angle of arrival* of a target signal consists essentially of noting the direction in which the antenna is pointing when the target is acquired. As was pointed out in Chap. 2, to improve the accuracy of the angular measurement, conical scanning or other techniques can be used.

When a pencil beam detects a target, the angular position of the target is known accurately, at least within the error of a beamwidth. However, if such a beam is used to search, it might take too long to cover the entire volume. Two fan beams, as described in Sec. 2-6, can accelerate the process. One beam is narrow in azimuth and wide in elevation. This beam is rotated through 360° (or less, if the target is in a known sector). When it detects a target, the azimuthal direction is known from the position of the antenna. The range is also known from the time of arrival. A second fan beam has the wide dimension in azimuth and is narrow in elevation. This beam moves up and down until a target is detected at the same range as the previously acquired signal. This beam then indicates the elevation of the target. The first fan beam is typical of a *search radar*. The second radar which determines elevation is sometimes called a *height finder*.

If two targets are at about the same range, but at slightly different angles, they can be separated if they are more than a beamwidth apart. If they are closer than this, echoes from both will return simultaneously from a single pulse and will appear in the receiver as one signal. The *angular resolution* of the radar, then, is the beamwidth.

3-6 DOPPLER

When a target is moving radially (that is, toward or away from the transmitter), the frequency of the returned echo is shifted from the original frequency by an amount dependent on the radial velocity of the target. The change in frequency is called the *Doppler frequency*, and it is approximately:

$$f_d = \frac{2f_t v_r}{c} \tag{3-10}$$

where f_d is the Doppler frequency

   f_t is the transmitted frequency

   v_r is the radial velocity of the target

   c is the speed of light, Eq. (3-9)

Thus, if the transmitted frequency is 10 000 MHz, and the velocity of the target toward the transmitter is 30 mph, the Doppler frequency is

$$f_d = \frac{2 \times 10^{10} \times 44}{984 \times 10^6} = 894 \text{ Hz}$$

(30 mph = 44 ft per second, 10 000 MHz = 10^{10} Hz)

Thus, the frequency of the returned signal is 894 Hz different from the transmitted frequency. If the target was approaching the transmitter, the Doppler would be added so that the returned frequency would be 10 000 000 894 Hz. If the target was moving away, the returned signal would be less than the transmitted frequency by the same amount.

If the returned signal is at a different frequency from the transmitted signal, the target must be moving radially. The Doppler frequency can be measured, and the velocity of the target can thus be determined by solving Eq. (3-10) for v_r. The radial velocity of the target is the rate at which the range of the target is changing, and it is usually referred to as the *range rate* of the target.

The measurement of Doppler frequency as well as range and angle makes it possible to pick out a moving target from larger, stationary masses. For example, the echo of a plane flying close to a mountain may be completely obscured by the echo from the mountain, but the plane's echo will be changed in frequency. A radar using Doppler can detect the plane easily.

3-7 BEACON EQUATION

A beacon is a form of radar which transmits a signal only when it receives a specific coded signal. In a radar beacon system, the conventional radar transmits a signal which is intercepted by the beacon. Instead of a reflection from the surface of the target, a transmitter on the beacon sends a return signal. The power and frequency of the return signal are fixed by the beacon transmitter and are not dependent on the target cross section, nor on the transmitted power. When the first signal is sent from the radar transmitter to the beacon, the radar is said to *interrogate* the beacon. The beacon *responds* only if it receives the correct "question" or coded transmission. The beacon is also called a *transponder*.

The radar equation (Eq. 3-8) for predicting range must be modified when applied to beacons. Since there are two distinct events, not necessarily at the same frequency, two equations must be used to predict the range. During the interrogation, the maximum range may be derived in a manner similar to that used to derive the radar equation. It is

$$R_{\max} = \left[\frac{P_T G_T A_B}{4\pi S_B} \right]^{1/2} \tag{3-11}$$

During the response, the maximum range is given by

$$R_{\max} = \left[\frac{P_B G_B A_e}{4\pi S_{\min}} \right]^{1/2} \tag{3-12}$$

In these two equations $R_{\max}$ is maximum range

P_T is the transmitted power from the interrogating radar

P_B is the power output of the beacon transmitter

G_T is the antenna gain of the interrogating radar

G_B is the gain of the beacon antenna

A_B is the effective aperture of the beacon antenna

A_e is the effective aperture of the radar receiving antenna

S_B is the minimum detectable signal of the beacon receiver

$S_{\min}$ is the minimum detectable signal of the radar receiver

If the values of $R_{\max}$ determined from Eqs. (3-11) and (3-12) are different, the lower value applies. In practice, the two values will be made approximately equal. In a typical application, the beacon may be located on a weather satellite to be interrogated from a high-powered radar on the ground. It responds with a coded signal which gives information about weather observations that have been gathered during its last revolution around the earth. The beacon must be small to fit on the satellite. Hence, its antenna will have a smaller aperture and gain than the earth-based radar's antenna. The transmitted power from the satellite is less than that from the interrogator, and the beacon receiver is not as sensitive as the radar receiver. Thus,

$$P_T > P_B$$

$$G_T > G_B$$

$$A_B < A_e$$

$$S_B > S_{\min}$$

3-8 EQUATION FOR BISTATIC RADAR

A *bistatic radar* has two separate antennas, one for transmitting and one for receiving, as opposed to a *monostatic radar* which has one antenna for both purposes. The term *bistatic*, however, is usually applied to a system in which the transmitter and receiver are widely separated as well as having separate antennas. Since the range between the transmitter and the target is usually different from the range between the target and receiver, the radar equation must be modified to apply. Instead of using the form for range, it is customary to use the form for received power, as in Eq. (3-7). For bistatic radars the received power is

$$P_R = \frac{P_T G_T G_R \lambda^2 \sigma_b}{(4\pi)^3 R_T^2 R_R^2} \tag{3-13}$$

Where P_R and P_T are the received power and the transmitted power, respectively

G_R and G_T are the gains of the receiver antenna and transmitter antenna

R_T is the range from the transmitter to the target

R_R is the range from the receiver to the target

λ is the wavelength

σ_b is the bistatic radar cross section, that is, it indicates the portion

of the transmitted power reflected toward the receiver

3-9 INTEGRATION

The various forms of the radar equation were derived on the basis of a single pulse transmitted and a single echo received. In any radar system, the transmitter emits many pulses during the time the antenna is pointing at a target, and many echoes are received. The succession of pulses transmitted and received is called a *pulse train*. If the energy in the echo from a single pulse is slightly below the noise level of the receiver, it will not be seen. However, if the energy from all the pulses in a train is added, the echo will stand out from the noise. *Integration* is the processing of the returned echoes to give an effective, or integrated, echo greater than any single one. Ideally, the integrated value should be the sum of all the signals in the train. To achieve this, the signals must be stored, as received, and added in phase before detection, which requires very complicated circuitry. This is called *predetection integration* or *coherent integration*. In most practical radars, integration takes place after detection and is known as *post-detection integration*. This integration takes place in the video circuit or display. Because of the nonlinearity of the detector circuit, the individual echoes do not add directly, so that the integrated value is less than the actual sum of the echo signals.

3-10 LOSSES

In any practical radar system, the achievable range is always substantially less than that calculated by using the radar equation (Eq. 3-8). There are many sources of loss in the system, and these losses reduce the energy of both the transmitted and the received signals. The overall loss is called the *system loss* and is the sum of all the losses (expressed in decibels).

The *RF transmission-line loss* is the attenuation due to the waveguides or coaxial lines and all components in the system. This includes directional couplers, duplexers, ferrite isolators, filters, etc., all of which have small but nonzero attenuation. If the sum of these losses between transmitter and antenna is only 1.0 db, the transmitted power at the antenna is reduced to 80 percent of its value at the transmitter. Similarly, the 1.0 db loss between antenna and receiver will cause another 20 percent loss. If the radar antenna is mismatched, there is additional loss due to reflection. A VSWR of 2 to 1 causes 11 percent of the power to be reflected. The *mismatch loss* is usually considered to be part of the transmission-line loss.

As the antenna scans by a target, a train of pulses will be transmitted and returned, as was explained in the preceding section. However, since the gain of the antenna refers only to a target on axis, the amplitudes of the returned pulses will be modulated by the shape of the antenna beam. If the value of antenna gain is used for all the pulses in the train, the result of the calculations of integration would be too large. The loss due to the beam shape is called the *beam-shape loss.*

In the integration process described in Sec. 3-9, it sometimes happens that, in addition to signals, samples of noise are included in the summation. This noise causes a reduction in signal-to-noise ratio, in effect reducing receiver sensitivity. The loss due to this degradation is called *collapsing loss.*

Propagation loss is attenuation of the signal during propagation in space. This includes effects of atmospheric absorption and reflection, as well as ground reflection and multipath transmissions.

Operator loss is a measure of the efficiency of the operator. In a typical system, an operator must watch one or more displays and pick out signals from noise. A trained operator can recognize a weaker signal better than an untrained operator. But even the trained operator will miss a weak signal when he is tired or under stress.

Each· value of loss may be expressed as a decimal fraction or in decibels. The system loss is the product of all the fractions or, when expressed logarithmically, the sum of the decibel values.

If the effect of the system loss is included in the radar equation, the equation will give a more accurate picture of practical achievable ranges. A *system loss factor* is placed in the denominator of Eq. (3-8), thus:

$$R_{\text{max}} = \left[\frac{P_T A_e^2 \sigma}{4\pi\lambda^2 S_{\text{min}}L} \right]^{1/4} \tag{3-14}$$

where L is a number greater than unity equivalent to the system loss in decibels. For example, if the system loss is 13 db, the loss factor L is 20. ($10 \log 20 = 13$.)

PROBLEMS

3-1. Express the radar equation (Eq. 3-8) in terms of antenna gain G instead of effective area A_e.

3-2. A perfectly conducting sphere is being radiated with a frequency such that its cross section is in the Rayleigh region. If the frequency is doubled, by what factor will the cross section change? Will the cross section increase or decrease?

ans: $16 = 12$ db

3-3. A target is 6 n.mi. from a radar which transmits a 3 μsec pulse. How much time will elapse between the transmission and reception of a pulse? What is the closest another target can be to this target and still be resolved?

ans: 74.4 μsec, 150 ft

3-4. Explain the difference between range resolution, azimuth resolution, and elevation resolution. (Draw sketches.)

3-5. A fan beam with a wide elevation angle is required to search a 90° sector. If the azimuth resolution is to be 5 percent of the sector, how wide (in degrees) should the azimuth beamwidth be?   *ans:* 4.5°

3-6. A C-band (f_T = 5000 MHz) Doppler radar is to detect all targets with radial velocities greater than 5 mph and less than 60 mph. What are the minimum and maximum Doppler frequencies which the radar must detect?

ans: 7.5 Hz, 900 Hz

3-7. A particular radar beacon has a minimum detectable signal which is four times greater than that of the radar receiver. What is the required ratio of radar power to beacon power for R_{max} to be the same in both directions if the radar frequency is half that of the beacon? (*Hint:* Use Eq. 2-2.)   *ans:* 16

3-8. A bistatic radar is positioned such that R_R is twice as great as R_T. How much more power must this system transmit for the received power to be equal to that of a monostatic system in which R_R is equal to R_T?   *ans:* 4 times

3-9. A certain radar requires a received power of 10^{-6} watts for detection. A single received pulse has 10^{-7} watts.

  (a) If the radar has perfect predetection integration, how many pulses must be integrated for detection?
  (b) If the radar employs post-detection integration with the total power equal to $\sqrt{N}P_R$ (N is the number of pulses integrated), how many pulses must be integrated?   *ans:* (a) 10, (b) 100

3-10. If no losses were encountered, a particular radar would have a range of 100 n.mi. If the total system loss is 12 db, what is the radar range? *ans:* 50 n.mi.

3-11. A device which is often used as a radar target is the corner reflector shown in Fig. P-3-11. When pointed directly at the radar, its cross section is

$$\sigma = \left(\frac{4}{3}\right)\frac{\pi a^4}{\lambda^2}$$

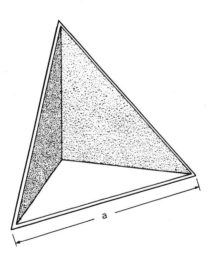

where a is the length of the side. Derive the range equation (similar to Eq. 3-8) for a corner reflector. If the radar frequency is doubled, by what factor will the range increase? How does this answer compare to a target with constant cross section?   *ans:* 2, $\sqrt{2}$

3-12. Derive equations similar to Eqs. (3-11) and (3-12) for a bistatic radar system which is used with a beacon. It will be necessary to use the symbols defined in conjunction with Eq. (3-13).

3-13. A radar is to be used in low-flying aircraft to detect telephone wires. What type of polarization would you recommend? Why?

Fig. P-3-11. Corner reflector.

3-14. A radar which transmits a 6 μsec pulse observes two targets at the same azimuth and elevation angle. One target is 2000 ft behind the other. Since this distance is less than the range resolution, only one pulse will be received. How long will this pulse be?   *ans:*   10 μsec

3-15. Describe the difference between bistatic and monostatic radar systems.

3-16. There are three types of scattering regions associated with radar targets. List them in the order they are encountered as the frequency is increased.

CHAPTER FOUR

C-W Radar

4-1 GENERAL

In Sec. 1-1 it was pointed out that a continuous transmission results in a continuous echo signal, and that it is thus impossible to tell which part of the echo is associated with any particular part of the transmission. It is also difficult to tell whether a received signal is actually an echo from a target or merely leakage from the transmitter, since they both have the same form and frequency. However, if the target is moving radially with respect to the transmitter, the echo signal will be shifted in frequency as described in Sec. 3-6. The *Doppler shift* or *Doppler frequency* is the difference in frequency between the transmitted and received signals. It is then possible to separate the echo from the transmitted signal on the basis of frequency.

4-2 DOPPLER

In Sec. 3-6, it was indicated that the Doppler frequency is

$$f_d = \frac{2f_t v_r}{c} \tag{4-1}$$

(This is the same as Eq. 3-10.) Since $c/f = \lambda$, another form of the equation is

$$f_d = \frac{2v_r}{\lambda} \tag{4-2}$$

where λ is the wavelength of the transmitted signal. It is important that all units be consistent when using and substituting in equations. Thus, in Eq. (4-1), if the velocity of the target, v_r, is given in miles per hour, c must also be in miles per hour, or both may be changed to feet per second or any

36

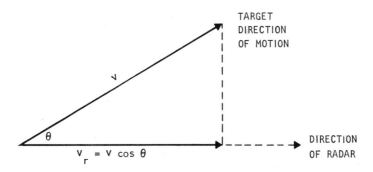

Fig. 4-1. Velocity components.

other consistent units. Similarly, in Eq. (4-2), if v_r is given in miles per hour, it should be changed so that the length dimension is the same as that for λ and the time dimension is 1 second, so that f_d will be in Hz (cycles per second). Thus, if λ is in centimeters, for example, v_r should be in centimeters per second.

The quantity v_r in Eqs. (4-1) and (4-2) is the *radial velocity* of the target. If the target is actually moving radially, that is, directly toward or away from the transmitter, the radial velocity is the same as the actual velocity. In general however, the target will be moving in a different direction. The radial velocity v_r then is the rate at which the distance to the target is changing, or the component of velocity in the radial direction. Figure 4-1 indicates the relationship between actual velocity and radial velocity. In the figure the target is moving at a velocity v in a direction θ from the direction of the radar. From the figure it is evident that

$$v_r = v \cos \theta \qquad (4\text{-}3)$$

When $\theta = 90°$, $v_r = 0$. This means that when a target is moving in a direction perpendicular to that of the transmitter, there is no Doppler shift.

4-3 C-W RADAR

A simple c-w radar, using Doppler, is shown in Fig. 4-2. The transmitter is connected to the antenna through a duplexer. Since the transmitter and receiver are both "on" continuously, the duplexer cannot be a switch as in a pulsed radar. Instead, a ferrite circulator or a magic tee may act as a duplexer.[1] In the magic tee, half the power is thrown away on transmission and half of what returns is lost on reception, but the circuit is simple and useful when there is more than enough power to spare.

---

[1] Cf. Wheeler, *Introduction to Microwaves*, pp. 193ff.

The transmitted signal at f_t (Fig. 4-2) arrives at the moving target and is changed in frequency by the motion so that the reflected signal is $f_t \pm f_d$. This echo is picked up by the antenna and passed to the detector by the duplexer. Some of the transmitted signal is deliberately made to leak into the detector to mix with the echo. The difference between the two signals appears at the output of the detector or mixer. This is simply the Doppler frequency.

The amplifier has two purposes. First, it must amplify the Doppler frequency so that it can be seen or heard on an indicator such as an oscillo-

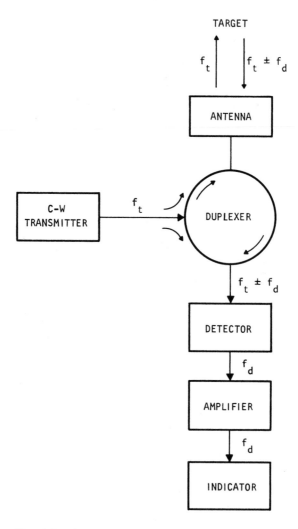

Fig. 4-2. C-W radar.

scope, earphones, a loudspeaker, or a meter. In the second place, the amplifier can be designed so that its frequency response will be highest in the region where Dopplers are expected. In particular, the low-frequency cutoff will be chosen to reject any d-c component caused by an echo from a stationary object.

4-4   ISOLATION

In Sec. 4-3 it was shown that some transmitter power must leak into the receiver to furnish a "local oscillator" signal for the echo to beat with. The amount of leakage must be controlled. In a high-power system, the leakage might damage the receiver if it were too high. Secondly, the transmitter signal carries with it noise components which tend to reduce the sensitivity of the mixer. Too much leakage, even though no receiver damage results, may still bring with it too much noise. In general, the detector, usually a crystal, has a best operating point, and the amount of leakage is controlled to provide just the right amount of d-c current in the detector.

Commercially available ferrite circulators have isolations ranging from 20 to 30 db. Thus, if a simple traffic monitoring radar has a 1-watt transmitter, a 30-db circulator would permit 1 milliwatt of power to get to the mixer. A good operating point for a mixer is in the $\frac{1}{2}$ to 1 milliwatt range, so this could be considered correct isolation. If the circulator had a higher isolation, the leakage might not be enough to *bias* the detector satisfactorily. In this case, leakage can be increased by providing a discontinuity, such as a small screw, to reflect some additional transmitter power to the detector. If the radar puts out a kilowatt, a 30-db circulator would allow 1 watt to get to the mixer. This is too much power for the leakage signal. Additional isolation can be achieved by feeding in a known sample of the transmitter power and adjusting the phase and amplitude of this sample to cancel some of the leakage signal. Where larger isolations are required, it is sometimes necessary to use two antennas, one for receiving and the other for transmitting. More than 70 db of isolation is easily achieved in this way.

4-5   RESOLUTION

The angular resolution of a c-w radar is determined by the antenna just as for a pulsed radar. This was explained in Sec. 3-5. Since the simple c-w Doppler radar gives no range information, there is no meaning to the term *range resolution* for this radar.

When two or more targets, moving at different radial velocities, are illuminated at one position of the antenna, the echoes will return at different frequencies and all will mix in the detector. The several Doppler shifts will all be amplified, and the output of the amplifier will consist of the various Doppler frequencies corresponding to the targets. If it is desired to separate these frequencies, a bank of Doppler filters may be used. These may be placed directly after the detector, in which case a high-gain, narrow-band amplifier can be placed after each filter. Or instead, the filter bank can follow the single broad-band amplifier. In either case, separate indicators are used for each Doppler frequency. The *velocity resolution* then is determined by the number of filters and the bandwidth of each. The number of targets that can be resolved at any one time cannot exceed the number of filters.

4-6 C-W IF RADAR

The simple receiver shown in Fig. 4-2 is like a superheterodyne with a zero intermediate frequency. It is simpler than a conventional superheterodyne, however, in that it requires neither a local oscillator nor an IF amplifier. However, the zero IF receiver is not as sensitive as the superheterodyne because the crystal mixer is noisier at the lower frequencies. The noise generated in the diode is approximately inversely proportional to the frequency $(1/f)$. For this reason it is called *one-over-f noise*. Thus, in the audio region, a diode introduces more noise than it does in the normal radar IF region (about 30 MHz). The addition of an IF capability to a c-w radar can increase the sensitivity by a factor of 1000.

Figure 4-3 shows a typical IF system. The transmitter output is fed to the antenna through a duplexer. This time there must be no leakage to the receiver. (If necessary, two separate antennas and no duplexer would be used.) A small part of the transmitted power is mixed with a 30 MHz signal (or any other frequency desired for the IF) and the output passed through a filter which allows only one sideband to pass. This sideband is now the *local oscillator* of the receiver. (It is also possible to replace the 30 MHz oscillator, mixer, and filter by a local oscillator exactly 30 MHz away from the c-w transmitter.) The received signal, with the Doppler added, mixes with the local oscillator in the detector to produce the intermediate frequency (30 MHz) plus and minus the Doppler frequency. After amplification, the second detector removes the IF, and only f_d appears at the output. This can be amplified as in Fig. 4-2 and fed to any kind of indicator.

As with the simple c-w radar, a bank of filters can be used to improve sensitivity and to resolve two or more signals coming from the same direction. The filter bank can be placed between the detector and IF amplifier, between the IF amplifier and second detector, or after the second detector. The last does not yield as good a sensitivity as the others, but only one second detector is necessary. If filters are used after the IF amplifier, a second detector must be used at the output of each filter.

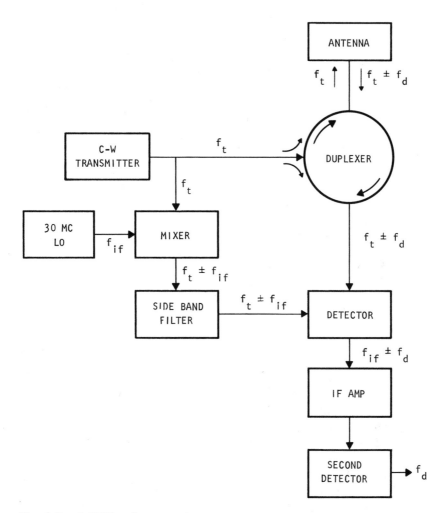

Fig. 4-3. C-W IF radar.

4-7 DIRECTION OF TARGET MOTION

An approaching target causes an increase in frequency while a receding one has a negative Doppler. The sign of the Doppler frequency cannot be determined by the receivers discussed thus far. In some cases it is necessary to know whether the target is approaching or receding. One method is a phasing method similar to that used in single-sideband circuits. A small part of the output of the transmitter is split equally and fed to two mixers, with the two signals being 90° out of phase. The received signal is also split, and half is fed to each mixer in phase. The relative phases of the two mixed outputs will indicate whether the Doppler is positive or negative.

If there is no hurry to ascertain the sign of the Doppler shift, there is a simpler method. Thus, presumably, a receding target will produce a weaker signal as time progresses, while an approaching target's signal gets stronger. Therefore, the amplitude of the signal as a function of time is an indication of direction. This method is particularly useful with rapidly moving targets.

4-8 APPLICATIONS OF C-W RADAR

The familiar traffic monitoring radar is a relatively simple c-w (continuous wave) radar. The velocity of an approaching automobile appears as a Doppler shift in the received signal. The frequency of the shift is measured and is related to the speed of the car by Eq. (4-1).

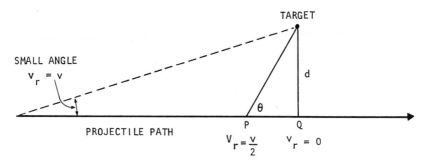

Fig. 4-4. Miss-distance indicator.

Another application is in a device called a *miss-distance indicator* which indicates how close a projectile comes to its target during testing runs. The geometry is shown in Fig. 4-4. A projectile is fired with a velocity v. A radar at the target detects the approaching projectile and notes its Doppler shift. At the start, the angle between the projectile path and the target is small, so that v_r is approximately equal to the true velocity. At some point P, the radial velocity will be half the original velocity, and at another point Q it will be zero. When $v_r = v/2$, it means that $\cos \theta = \frac{1}{2}$. Therefore, $\theta = 60°$. The time span from P to Q is noted and is multiplied by the known velocity v to yield the distance PQ. From trigonometry, the *miss-distance d* is equal to this distance times $\sqrt{3}$.

4-9 FM–C-W RADAR

The most serious limitation of the simple c-w radar is that it furnishes no information about the range of the target. Since both the transmitter and receiver are working continuously, and every part of the echo from a target looks like every other part, it is impossible to associate a particular instant in the echo signal with a specific part of the transmission. One method of obtaining range information from a c-w radar is by using frequency modulation (FM). The transmitter emits a signal continuously, but the frequency is changed in a known fashion. When the echo returns, it is at the frequency of the original transmission (assuming, for the moment, that the target is stationary), while the transmitter is now radiating at a new frequency. The difference in frequency, then, is a measure of the range.

The modulation can be sinusoidal, sawtooth, triangular, or of any shape, as long as the frequency is changing and the rate of change is known. A useful and simple form is triangular modulation, as illustrated in Fig. 4-5. This is a plot of frequency as a function of time. The solid line represents the transmitted frequency. The dotted line represents the frequency of the received echo from a stationary target. It has exactly the same form as the transmitted signal except that it is delayed by a time T. Since time is equal to distance divided by velocity, if the target is at a range R and the signal travels at the speed of light c, then

$$T = \frac{2R}{c} \qquad (4\text{-}4)$$

At any moment of time, t_x, if the returned signal is compared to the signal which is being transmitted at that moment, there will be a frequency difference which will be constant throughout the time interval (except at the turn-around points). The frequency difference is directly proportional to the range R.

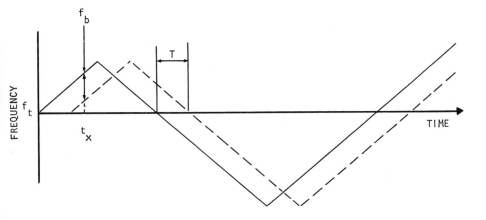

Fig. 4-5. Triangular FM.

Figure 4-6 is a block diagram of a simple FM–c-w radar. It is shown with two antennas, but it is possible to use a single antenna and a duplexer. The transmitter puts out a signal like the solid line in Fig. 4-5. A small portion of this leaks or is fed into the mixer as a reference signal. The returned signal is shifted in frequency by an amount f_b. The reference and echo signals beat in the mixer to produce the *beat frequency* f_b, which is amplified. The frequency counter measures the frequency f_b, and the indicator expresses f_b in range.

If the target is moving, the returned signal will also have a Doppler frequency added to it. If the target is approaching, the Doppler shift will have a positive sign. In effect, the dotted line of Fig. 4-5 will be raised vertically due to the addition of f_d, but not shifted in time. Thus, on the upward portion of the FM, f_b will be decreased; but on the downward portion, f_b will be increased. The net effect is to produce two alternating beat frequencies: a smaller f_{b_1} on the upward modulation and a larger f_{b_2} on the down slope.

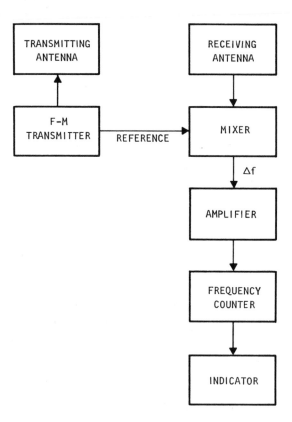

Fig. 4-6. FM–C-W radar.

It is evident that

$$f_{b_1} = f_b - f_d \tag{4-5}$$

and

$$f_{b_2} = f_b + f_d \tag{4-6}$$

where f_b is the beat frequency that would exist if the target were stationary and f_d is the Doppler frequency due to the radial velocity. By measuring the two alternating beat frequencies, f_{b_1} and f_{b_2}, it is now possible to determine f_b to get range and f_d to get velocity. Thus, by adding Eqs. (4-5) and (4-6),

$$f_b = \frac{f_{b_1} + f_{b_2}}{2} \tag{4-7}$$

and by subtracting,

$$f_d = \frac{f_{b_2} - f_{b_1}}{2} \tag{4-8}$$

4-10　APPLICATION OF FM–C-W RADAR

The FM–c-w radar is most useful for measuring short ranges where the target is large. A typical application is in a radar altimeter. The earth presents a large target so that a strong echo is obtained. This permits the use of a small, low-power transmitter and a low-gain antenna on the altimeter in the plane, where space and weight are at a premium.

PROBLEMS

4-1. A useful number is Doppler frequency per mile per hour of target radial velocity (f_D/v_r). Compute this number for

(a) $\lambda = 0.1$ ft　　　　　　　　(b) $\lambda = 0.2$ ft

(c) $\lambda = 1.0$ ft　　　　*ans:*　(a) 30 Hz/mph, (b) 15 Hz/mph, (c) 3 Hz/mph

4-2. What is the major advantage of the receiver of Fig. 4-3 over that shown in Fig. 4-2? Point out two disadvantages.

4-3. A Doppler radar transmitting a frequency of 10 000 MHz is located at point O in Fig. P-4-3. A target moves along line AB with a speed of 20 mph. Sketch the value of the Doppler frequency as a function of time. What type of Doppler vs. time curve would be obtained if the radar were located at point B?

4-4. Assume that the radar shown in Fig. 4-2 operates at a frequency of 5000 MHz. It is to detect targets moving as slowly as 3 mph. At what low frequency should the amplifier cut off?　　　　　　　　　　　　　　　　　*ans:*　45 Hz

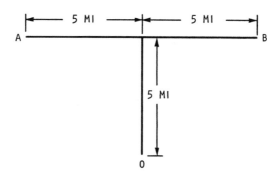

Fig. P-4-3.   Problem geometry.

4-5. A particular mixer requires 2 milliwatts of reference signal power for best operation. If the transmitter output power is 5 watts, how much isolation must be provided?   *ans:*   34 db

4-6. Draw block diagrams of the receiver of Fig. 4-2 showing two different ways that Doppler filter banks can be installed.

4-7. A Doppler radar operating at 10 000 MHz is to have a velocity resolution of 5 mph and is to cover a range of target speeds from 5 to 100 mph. How many filters must the bank contain? What should the bandwidth of each filter be?

ans: 19, 150 Hz

4-8. A Doppler radar with $\lambda = 1$ ft observes two targets. One is moving directly toward the radar with a speed of 100 mph while the other is moving directly away with the same speed. What will be the frequency difference between the two received signals? Which target will produce the higher frequency signal?

ans: 600 Hz

4-9. For a given Doppler filter bank, can the velocity resolution be made smaller by increasing or decreasing the transmitted frequency? Explain your answer.

4-10. How could the IF amplifier of the receiver of Fig. 4-3 be designed so that only targets moving toward the radar would be detected? What is a practical limitation on this technique?

4-11. A radar of the type shown in Fig. 4-3 operates at 10 000 MHz. The IF amplifier is designed to pass all signals between 4 mph and 30 mph and reject all others. However, the 30 MHz oscillator can drift by as much as ± 240 Hz. Explain how this drift can affect the received signals.

4-12. The miss-distance indicator of Fig. 4-4 could also be designed such that P is the point where $v_r = v/\sqrt{2}$. For this system, by what factor must the distance PQ be multiplied to yield the miss-distance d?   *ans:*   1

4-13. What target property determines

(a) f_d in Fig. 4-2

(b) Δf in Fig. 4-6

How are these two properties related?

4-14. An FM–c-w radar transmits the signal shown in Fig. 4-5. If the frequency changes 2000 Hz every microsecond, what will the output frequency be due to a target which is 8000 ft away from the radar?   *ans:*   32 000 Hz

4-15. An FM–c-w radar uses triangular modulation with a basic frequency of 10 000 MHz. For a certain target, the beat frequency is 5120 Hz for upward modulation and 4880 Hz for downward modulation. What is the radial speed of the target? Is the target approaching or leaving the radar?   *ans:*   4 mph

4-16. An FM–c-w radar whose block diagram is shown in Fig. 4-6 transmits a triangular frequency modulation in which the frequency changes 1000 Hz every microsecond. Show how a filter bank can be included in the radar to produce a range resolution of 1000 ft. What should the bandwidth of each filter be?

                                                     ans: 2000 Hz

CHAPTER FIVE

Pulsed-Doppler Radar

5-1 MOVING-TARGET-INDICATION (MTI)

In a simple c-w radar, it is impossible to detect a stationary target. By making use of the Doppler shift, the c-w radar is able to detect moving targets, but can furnish no range information. On the other hand, a pulsed radar can detect both moving targets and stationary targets, and can furnish range information for either by noting the time interval between the transmitted and received signals. Furthermore, if a target is moving, the blip on the PPI will move as the target position changes, so that the simple pulsed radar can furnish information about target motion without using Doppler. On the face of it then, it appears that the use of Doppler shift in a pulsed radar is an unnecessary complication.

It should be remembered that a radially moving target causes a Doppler shift, whether the radar uses the information or not. If the information can be used profitably, the radar should be equipped to sense the Doppler. In point of fact, sensing the Doppler shift permits the pulsed radar to detect a weak signal from a moving target in the presence of strong signals from stationary targets. A typical application occurs when an enemy plane is flying close to a hill. The echoes from the plane and the hill arrive at the radar at approximately the same time; since the hill has a much larger radar cross section, the echo from the plane is hidden. By using the Doppler shift and special circuitry, however, the echo from the stationary object, the hill, is canceled, and the moving target is easily located. This is called *moving-target-indication* or MTI, and a pulsed radar with this capability is called a *pulsed Doppler radar* or an *MTI radar*. The term *clutter* applies to both the echoes from the stationary targets and to the stationary targets themselves. In practice, an MTI radar can discern a moving target in the presence of clutter hundreds of times as strong.

5-2 PULSED-OSCILLATOR MTI

In a pulsed radar system, the transmitter is turned on and off by the modulator at a fixed repetition rate and for a fixed duration. If the oscillator is a magnetron, the phase of the RF signal at the start of a pulse may be anything from $\backsim$ 360°. In an MTI radar the phase of the returned echo signal must be compared with the phase of a reference signal. Echoes from fixed targets will have fixed phase differences from the reference signal, and these returns can be canceled out; but moving targets will produce echoes with continuously changing phase (at the Doppler frequency).

It is necessary that the reference signal be locked in phase with the transmitted signal. The two signals are then said to be *coherent*, and the system is referred to as *coherent MTI*. Despite the fact that the phase of the oscillator may be completely random, it is possible to devise a circuit which will furnish a reference circuit coherent with the transmission. This is shown in Fig. 5-1. The oscillator in this figure may be a magnetron which is modulated by the pulses. The pulsed signal is radiated from the antenna after passing through the duplexer. The duplexer is usually some form of T-R tube. The *STALO*, or stable local oscillator, provides a very stable RF signal which differs from the transmitted frequency by the intermediate frequency. In other words, it functions simply as a local oscillator in a typical superheterodyne circuit. The received echo from the antenna passes through the duplexer to the receiver mixer, where it is combined with the STALO signal to produce the IF signal.

The *COHO*, or coherent local oscillator, furnishes a reference signal which is coherent with the transmitted signal. The COHO oscillates at the intermediate frequency. At the beginning of each pulse, a small part of the signal from the RF oscillator and part of the STALO signal are mixed in the locking mixer (or lock-pulse mixer). The output of this mixer during the pulse sets the phase of the COHO, which then oscillates freely until the phase is reset on the next pulse. In this way the COHO signal is always coherent with the transmitted signal and can be used as a reference for the echo.

The IF signal out of the receiver mixer is amplified in the IF amplifier and then compared in phase with the coherent reference signal from the COHO. The output of the phase detector is proportional to the phase difference between these two signals. Figure 5-2(a) shows the output of the phase detector as a function of time for successive pulses. The fixed targets look the same for all pulses, but the phase of the moving targets is continuously changing. The output of the phase detector is now passed through a delay line and canceler. In effect, all signals are delayed one inter-pulse interval and are then subtracted from the next pulse. The signals which appear the

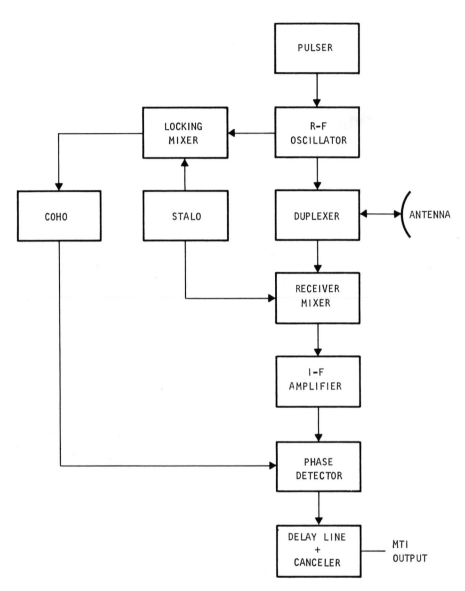

Fig. 5-1. Pulsed-oscillator MTI.

same for all pulses (the fixed target signals), are thus canceled. The result is shown in Fig. 5-2(b), where only the echoes from moving targets remain.

The signals in Fig. 5-2(b) are *bipolar*. That is, the voltages are both positive and negative. If this were used to operate a display which depended on the average voltage, there would be no indication because the average

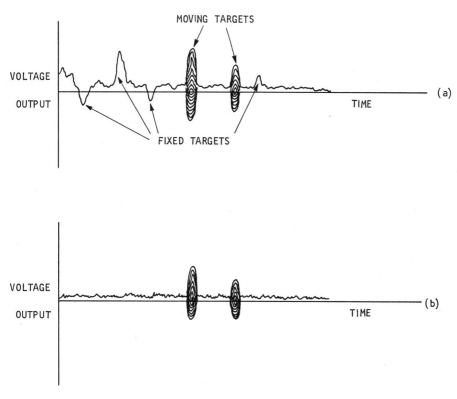

Fig. 5-2. Output of phase detector.

voltage is about zero. Thus, the output in Fig. 5-2(b) is usually rectified before it is used for displays. The signals could also be applied to an audio amplifier for aural detection.

5-3 NONCOHERENT MTI

An MTI radar which operates on amplitude variations instead of phase does not need a coherent reference. Hence, it is called *noncoherent*. In this system the echo from the moving target is compared to the echoes from fixed targets, and in the canceler, the echoes from fixed targets are removed. The system is much simpler than the coherent MTI radar, but it does require the presence of fixed targets. In effect, the echoes from the fixed targets provide the reference signal.

Area MTI is a form of noncoherent pulsed radar in which the Doppler shift is ignored. The PPI display screen has long persistence, and moving targets thus appear to have wakes or tails while the fixed targets are stationary and sharp. An experienced operator gets accustomed to ignoring the sharp signals and "sees" only the moving targets.

5-4 PULSED-AMPLIFIER MTI

The main problem with the circuit of Fig. 5-1 is the random pulse of the RF oscillator, which makes it extremely difficult to lock the COHO to the transmitted pulse. With the advent of microwave power amplifiers such as the power klystrons, a more dependable circuit was developed. This is called *pulsed-amplifier MTI* and is shown in Fig. 5-3. In this circuit, the COHO and STALO are both very stable c-w oscillators. The COHO operates at the intermediate frequency. The two oscillator outputs are combined in the transmitter mixer, and the sum of the two frequencies is then fed to the power amplifier to become the transmitted frequency. Thus, the transmitted signal derives its phase from the COHO (as well as the STALO), instead of the other way around as in the pulsed-oscillator system. The power amplifier is modulated by the pulser just as the oscillator was modulated in Fig. 5-1. The rest of the circuit is identical with that of the pulsed-oscillator circuit.

5-5 BLIND SPEEDS

In Fig. 5-2(a), the fixed targets appear as steady signals, whereas the moving targets fluctuate at the Doppler frequency. However, if a target is moving at such a speed that the phase change from one pulse to the next is exactly a multiple of 360°, then the echo will be stationary on the voltage-time plot of Fig. 5-2(a). This occurs when the Doppler frequency is exactly equal to the pulse repetition frequency or a multiple of it. When a target is moving at such a velocity, its echo will be canceled along with the echoes from fixed targets. Hence, the velocity is called a *blind speed*.

The Doppler frequency was given in Eq. (4-2) and is repeated here:

$$f_d = \frac{2v_r}{\lambda} \tag{5-1}$$

Setting f_d equal to a multiple of the pulse repetition frequency f_r, and solving for v_r:

$$v_r = \frac{nf_r\lambda}{2} \qquad n = 1, 2, 3, \ldots \tag{5-2}$$

where v_r and λ are in the same units. The values of v_r obtained from Eq. (5-2) are the *blind speeds*. That is, targets moving at these radial velocities will not be seen by the MTI radar.

From Eq. (5-2), it is evident that the first blind speed ($n = 1$) can be increased by an increase in the repetition frequency or an increase in λ (lowering frequency) or both. In practice, if it is important to avoid blind speeds,

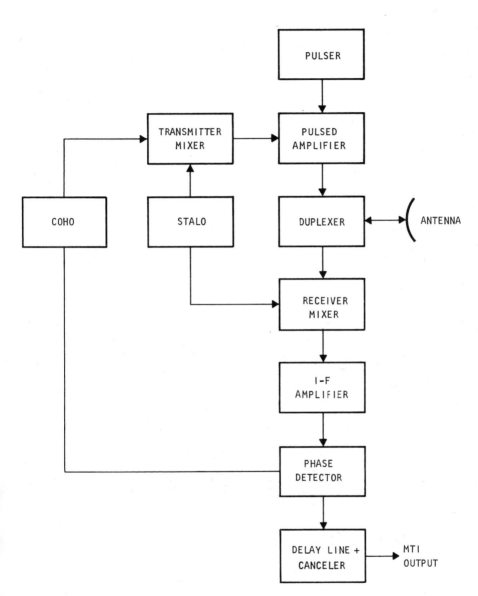

Fig. 5-3.   Pulse-amplifier MTI.

the repetition frequency is increased to a value which makes the first blind speed larger than the velocities of interest.

It is possible to minimize the occurrence of blind speeds in the range of interest by varying the pulse repetition frequency. In practice, every second transmitted pulse is delayed by a small interval. The result is a *staggered p.r.f.* as shown in Fig. 5-4. The shorter interval, t_1, produces a blind speed

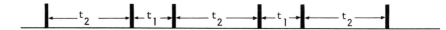

Fig. 5-4. Staggered pulse repetition frequency.

which is higher than that of the longer interval, t_2. (A shorter interval implies a higher p.r.f.) A blind speed due to one of these intervals will usually not be blind for the other. The *stagger ratio* is the ratio of the smaller to the larger interval or t_1/t_2. A disadvantage of this technique is some loss in sensitivity.

5-6 DELAY LINE AND CANCELER

The delay-line and canceler technique indicated in Figs. 5-1 and 5-3 was one of the first methods of removing the stationary target returns in an MTI radar. The delay line was required to delay the signal until the next pulse arrived. Thus, if the p.r.f. was 1000, the delay would have to be $\frac{1}{1000}$ second or 1 millisecond. At radio frequencies, this means a delay line equivalent to 984 000 ft, an unwieldy size. To simplify the problem, the RF signal is converted to an acoustic signal and put through an acoustic delay line, which is a much smaller device for the same equivalent delay. The acoustic signal is then converted back to RF.

As returns from each pulse come out of the phase detector, part of the output is delayed and then fed to the canceler, while the rest is fed to the canceler directly. The delayed portion always arrives, then, at the same time as the undelayed portion of the next pulse. Since the delay line has considerable loss, the delayed portion must be amplified or the undelayed part attenuated so that the two are about equal in the canceler.

The cancelation produced by the delay line and canceler will be complete for stationary targets, but not for slow-moving targets such as clouds or swaying trees on a hillside. To broaden the width of the cancelation notch, that is, to eliminate slow-moving targets as well as stationary ones, a second delay line and canceler can be added in series with the first. However, there is also an added disadvantage in that the blind speeds are also "broadened."

That is, a wider cancelation (in frequency) for slow-moving targets results effectively in blind speeds at harmonics of the slow-moving target velocities.

5-7 RANGE GATES AND FILTERS

In Fig. 5-2, it is evident that the location of the signal on the horizontal axis is a measure of time of arrival, just as on an A-scope. Thus, the range information inherent in a pulsed radar system is preserved in the MTI radar. If, instead of the delay-line-canceler approach, a simple Doppler filter were used, range information would be lost, and the system would become a pulsed version of a simple c-w Doppler system.

One method of using Doppler filters and still preserving range information is by utilizing range gates. A *gate* is simply a switch which opens and closes at preset times. A *range gate*, then, is a switch which opens at a time coinciding with a prescribed range and closes at a set time later. For example, if a range gate is set to pass echoes from all targets between 10 and 11 miles away, the gate will open 124 μsec after the transmitted pulse (assuming 12.4 μsec per mile, as indicated in Sec. 3-4) and will close 12.4 μsec later. By quantizing range into small, conveniently handled sizes, a bank of range gates can be designed. The range gates replace the delay line and canceler in Figs. 5-1 and 5-3. Each range gate is then followed by a bank of Doppler filters. In this way, range information, at least within specified quantization, is obtained by noting the particular gate through which a specified signal passed. Doppler information is obtained from the filter outputs. Fixed target echoes may pass through appropriate range gates but will be filtered out by the Doppler filters.

5-8 PULSED-DOPPLER RADAR

The MTI radars heretofore described are, of course, pulsed-Doppler radars in that they are pulsed and utilize the Doppler shift. The terms *pulsed-Doppler* and *MTI* are sometimes used interchangeably. However, strictly speaking, an MTI radar is one which uses Doppler to detect a moving target and reject signals from fixed targets, while a pulsed-Doppler radar uses Doppler for other purposes as well.

In general, a pulsed-Doppler radar (as distinguished from an MTI radar) will have range gates and Doppler filters rather than a delay line and canceler. To eliminate blind speeds, the pulsed-Doppler radar will use a high pulse repetition frequency. The p.r.f. will be chosen high enough to make the first blind speed higher than the expected target velocities. Use of a high p.r.f. results in range ambiguities, as was mentioned in Sec. 1-2. The range ambiguity can be resolved by the use of a staggered pulse repetition frequency.

PROBLEMS

5-1. What is the meaning of the word *coherent* when referring to coherent MTI?

5-2. What is the difference between the STALO and COHO in Fig. 5-1?

5-3. A target is moving away from a coherent MTI radar at a speed such that the phase increases 90° between successive pulses. Illustrate the phase detector output. (Assume the initial phase difference is 0°.)

5-4. Could a noncoherent MTI radar be used for aircraft detection? Why? Could it be used for the detection of moving personnel and vehicles? Why?

5-5. In Fig. 5-1, assume the magnetron frequency is 9375 MHz and the COHO frequency is 30 MHz. The radar observes an approaching target which has a radial velocity of 30 n.mi. per hour. What is the transmitted frequency? What is the received frequency? What is the frequency of the mixer output signal? At what frequency must the STALO operate?

ans: 9375 MHz, 9375 MHz + 970 Hz, 30 MHz + 970 Hz, 9345 MHz or 9405 MHz

5-6. In Fig. 5-3 assume that the STALO frequency is 9345 MHz and the COHO frequency is 30 MHz. The radar observes an approaching target which has a radial velocity of 30 n.mi. per hour. What is the transmitted frequency? What is the received frequency? What is the mixer output frequency? Compare these answers to those of Prob. 5-5.

5-7. Express the blind speeds (Eq. 5-2) in terms of the maximum unambiguous range. (*Hint:* See Prob. 1-3.) For a fixed wavelength, how does the first blind speed ($n = 1$) change as the maximum range is increased?

5-8. Using the results of Prob. 5-7, calculate the first blind speed of a radar operating at 10 000 MHz with a maximum range of 200 n.mi.   *ans:*   20 ft/second

5-9. It is often convenient to express Eq. (5-2) as

$$v_r = Knf_r\lambda \qquad n = 1, 2, \ldots$$

where v_r has units of n.mi. per hour, f_r has units of pps, and λ has units of ft. Determine the value of K. What is the value of K if λ has units of centimeters?

ans: 0.296, 0.0098

5-10. What is the advantage of using a staggered p.r.f.? List two disadvantages.

5-11. The input to a delay-line canceler is the sequence

$$\ldots, +1, 0, -1, 0, \ldots$$

where the basic sequence is repeated continually. What is the output sequence of the canceler? What is the output of a second canceler which is added in series with the first?   *ans:* $\ldots, +1, -1, -1, +1, \ldots$, $\ldots, 0, -2, 0, +2, \ldots$

5-12. A range-gated MTI radar with a pulse duration of 6.2 μsec is to detect all targets between 1 mile and 20 miles away. If the range gates are open for an amount of time equal to the pulse duration, how many range gates are needed?   *ans:*   38

5-13. What is the difference between MTI radar and pulsed-Doppler radar?

5-14.   If the phase of the COHO in Fig. 5-1 is not locked perfectly, but varies from pulse to pulse, how will the performance of the system be affected?

5-15.   If the frequency of the STALO in Fig. 5-3 changes between the time the pulse is transmitted and the time it is received, how would the performance of the system be affected?

CHAPTER SIX

Types of Radars

6-1 FUNCTIONS OF A RADAR SET

Basically, a radar set must perform one of two functions. Either it must search for a target or, having located a target, it must follow it. A radar that hunts for a target is called a *search* or *acquisition radar*, and when it finds a target, it is said to *acquire* it. During search, the radar operator may or may not know that a target is in the volume of space being searched. Thus a weather radar on an airplane is used to look for storms in the plane's path, whether or not they exist. On the other hand, when a satellite is in orbit, a radar acquires it every time it passes overhead, the time of passage well-known in advance.

A radar that follows a moving target is called a *tracker* or *tracking radar*. To be able to do this, the tracking radar must sense the direction of motion and move so as to keep the transmitted beam always pointing toward the target. A tracking radar which constantly follows the target is said to be tracking *continuously*. If the angular position is simply sampled on each scan of the tracker, it is called a *track-while-scan radar*. Usually, the term *tracker* means a continuously tracking radar unless track-while-scan is specified.

Tracking implies following the angular position of the target in azimuth and elevation. This is called tracking *in angle*. If the tracker also supplies continuous range information, it is said to track *in range* as well as in angle. Similarly, if Doppler shift is noted continuously, the radar is said to track *in Doppler*, also. In a *track-while-scan* radar, it is also possible to track in range or in Doppler, as well as in angle.

6-2 SEARCH RADAR

When looking for a target or targets, an acquisition radar frequently has to cover a large volume of space. If the radar employed a narrow pencil beam and scanned the volume of space systematically, it would take too long to cover the total volume. Conceivably, a desired target such as a plane could fly through one portion of the volume while the pencil beam was pointing elsewhere. Consequently, fan beams, described in Sec. 3-5, are frequently used in search radars. One beam is used to measure azimuth and the other measures elevation. If several targets are detected, they are correlated according to range. That is, an azimuth echo and an elevation echo coming from the same distance are assumed to come from the same target. The search radar can acquire many targets at different ranges simultaneously.

If the volume to be searched is limited, it is possible to use a pencil beam efficiently for acquisition. For example, a weather radar on a plane must locate storms only in the path that the plane will take. The pencil beam then needs to scan only a very small angle to cover the volume of interest. In such a case, the same radar can be used for search and for track, but in many applications, the search and tracking functions are delegated to separate radars.

6-3 TRACKING RADAR

A tracking radar uses a pencil beam which is pointed at the known position of the target after it is acquired. If the target moves, an *error signal* is produced in the receiver of the tracking radar. This error signal indicates the direction of motion and operates a servo to move the tracker. As the tracker moves in the indicated direction, the error signal decreases and becomes zero when the tracker is pointing directly at the target. The error signal is produced by one of the methods indicated in Secs. 2-8, 2-9, and 2-10 (conical scanning, monopulse, or sequential lobing).

In conical scanning (Sec. 2-8), there is no modulation on the received signal when the target is directly on *boresight*, that is, straight ahead. When the target moves off the beam, a modulation is produced at the nutation rate. The modulation, then, is the error signal. The *phase* of the modulation indicates the position of the beam which produces the largest return and thus indicates the direction in which the antenna must be moved. The error signal is picked off in a separate circuit, is amplified, and is fed to servos which position the antenna. Usually two servos are used to move the antenna, one in azimuth and the other in elevation.

Sequential lobing (Sec. 2-10) also produces modulation as an error signal. In practice, two error signals are used. One is produced by the top and bottom beams and is used to drive the elevation servo. The modulation from the other two beams drives the azimuth servo.

In monopulse (Sec. 2-9), the two beams are always "on" simultaneously. The error signal is the difference between the two. In *amplitude monopulse*, the error signal is a difference in amplitude, while in *phase monopulse* it is a difference in phase. In a four-feed monopulse system, two error signals are used, one for azimuth and one for elevation. They may both be amplitude differences, both phase differences, or one of each.

6-4 TRACK-WHILE-SCAN

In a track-while-scan radar, the antenna beam scans by the target on each revolution or each scan. During the brief interval that the target is illuminated, the angular position is noted. On successive scans the position will change, and it is thus possible to approximate the track of the target and even extrapolate its future position. For example, if successive positions of the target are noted on the face of a PPI with a grease pencil, the succession of dots will indicate the track of the target.

One advantage of track-while-scan is that it makes possible the tracking of several targets with a single radar. Contrasted to this, the continuous tracker follows a single target and ignores all others. The track-while-scan radar can even acquire new targets while it is following others.

6-5 SIMPLE RADARS

Radar principles are frequently used in rather elementary form for purposes other than tracking or acquisition. The *Doppler navigator* is a c-w Doppler radar which is used to determine the velocity of an airplane relative to the earth, that is, the ground speed of the plane. In simple form, a c-w radar in the plane points forward at an angle of 45° to the horizontal, as shown in Fig. 6-1. The target in this case is the earth. An echo from the ground returns to the plane with a Doppler shift dependent on the relative

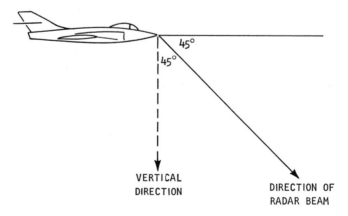

Fig. 6-1. Doppler navigator.

speed between the plane and the ground. It should be noted that the radar cannot distinguish between the case when the radar is stationary and the target is moving, and the case when the target is stationary and the radar is moving. The Doppler shift will be dependent on the radial velocity and the wavelength of propagation as indicated in Eq. (4-3), which is repeated here:

$$f_d = \frac{2v_r}{\lambda} \tag{6-1}$$

The radial velocity, in turn, is given by Eq. (4-3), which is

$$v_r = v \cos \theta \tag{6-2}$$

In this case, θ is $45° = 0.707$. Thus

$$f_d = \frac{1.414v}{\lambda} \tag{6-3}$$

Solving for v, the velocity of the plane with respect to ground is

$$v = \frac{\lambda f_d}{1.414} \tag{6-4}$$

If the angle θ is more than $45°$, the returned signal would be stronger, but the Doppler shift would be less because of the smaller radial velocity. The value of θ is a convenient compromise between range sensitivity and Doppler shift.

The traffic monitoring radar and miss-distance indicator described in Sec. 4-8 are other examples of relatively simple radar applications which are neither search nor acquisition. The radar altimeter described in Sec. 4-10 is a simple form of acquisition radar. The target is the earth, and when it is acquired, only the range is measured.

6-6 FIRE CONTROL RADARS

The error signal produced in a tracking radar is used to point the antenna beam at the target continuously, as was described in Sec. 6-3. The same error signal can be applied to point a gun at the target as well. The radar then controls the direction of firing and is called a *fire control radar*. The gun is said to be *slaved* to the radar.

In a typical ground or shipborne application, an acquisition radar searches for enemy planes. When one is found, location information is furnished a tracking radar, which then tracks the plane. The anti-aircraft guns are slaved to the tracking radar and are fired when the enemy plane comes within range.

In the early days of World War II, it was sufficient to have the guns point in the same direction as the antenna beam. However, as planes became faster, it became evident that the guns had to point ahead of the beam since, during the time it took for the shells to reach the plane's altitude, the plane would have moved too far to be hit. In a modern fire control radar, the information from the tracking radar is fed to a computer. This includes range and angle measurements and also the rate at which the angle is changing. The computer then calculates the trajectory of the plane and combines this with the velocity of the shells to predict a target intercept point. The anti-aircraft guns are slaved to the computer, which points them so that the shells will arrive at the intercept point at the same time as the enemy plane. The computer circuits are usually termed *logic circuits*.

A fire control radar which is carried in an airplane to control the plane's guns against an enemy plane is called an *airborne interceptor*. There is insufficient room to spare in a plane to afford the luxury of two separate radars, one for search and one for tracking. Consequently, in an airborne interceptor, both functions are combined in a single radar. The search function is performed with a pencil beam in this case, but the anticipated direction of arrival of enemy planes is generally known, so that the volume to be scanned is comparatively small. When a target is detected, the radar stops scanning and locks on the target, tracking it continuously until it is shot down or moves out of radar range.

6-7 EARLY WARNING RADAR

As its name implies, an *early warning radar* is a long-range acquisition radar which searches for enemy action at a distance in order to provide warning in time for effective counteraction. A typical example is in the detection of firings of intercontinental ballistic missiles (ICBM) at distances greater than 2000 miles so that anti-missile missiles may be launched in time to intercept them. Early warning radars are characterized by high power, large antennas, and frequencies in the u.h.f. region where atmospheric attenuation is low.

When the early warning radar is used specifically to search for planes at long ranges, rather than missiles, it is called an *aircraft-surveillance radar*. This is usually a large, ground-based radar for detecting enemy planes before they come close enough to inflict damage. Since planes do not travel as fast as ICBM's, the aircraft-surveillance radar is not required to acquire targets at as great a range as the early warning radar looking for ICBM's, but the principles of both are similar.

6-8 AIR-TRAFFIC CONTROL RADAR

An aircraft-surveillance radar can also be used to keep track of friendly planes. This is called *air-traffic control*. The range of an air-traffic control radar depends on the distance that it is necessary to monitor in order to insure safety. The radar must search the required volume, and targets are usually displayed on a PPI. Once a plane is acquired, the radar operates effectively as a track-while-scan radar.

Close to an airport, planes are assigned altitudes and are in voice communication with the control tower to report their altitudes. Thus, scanning can be done by a fan beam which searches only in azimuth. The track-while-scan function, also, need be done only in azimuth.

In a large airport, an important part of air-traffic control is monitoring the movement of planes and trucks on the ground as well as planes in the air. This is accomplished with a pulsed radar mounted on the control tower. To get the required resolution, the azimuth beamwidth is quite small, usually less than half a degree. The shape of the beam in elevation is tailored to return approximately equal power from all parts of the field. In effect, the energy is radiated in a fan beam with all portions of the field in the fan irradiated equally. This type of beam is called a *cosecant-squared pattern* since the power level varies as the square of the cosecant of the vertical angle. An important characteristic of this pattern is that targets at a constant altitude are irradiated equally, independent of range.

Since all targets are relatively close in this application, a high repetition rate is used. Also, since it is necessary to separate objects on the ground which are close together, high resolution is achieved by short pulses. A PPI is used for display and all targets appear, both moving and stationary.

6-9 WEATHER-AVOIDANCE RADAR

As its name implies, a *weather-avoidance radar* is used in a plane to detect the presence of turbulence and to enable the pilot to change his course to avoid the storm. In effect, a weather-avoidance radar searches for rain which is closely associated with turbulence. The frequency of the radar is chosen so that the raindrops have as large a radar cross section as possible. However, another consideration is the increased attenuation of higher frequencies. Thus, at X-band (near 10 000 MHz) the raindrops have a larger cross section than at C-band (about 5000 MHz), but the C-band radar has higher sensitivity because of the increased attenuation of the atmosphere at X-band. Most commercial airlines use C-band weather-avoidance radars.

6-10 BEACONS

Beacons were described briefly in Sec. 3-7. A *beacon* is a form of radar which transmits a signal only when it receives a specific coded signal. A conventional radar transmits a signal which is received by the beacon. This signal is coded by pulse width, pulse grouping, pulse repetition rate, or any combination of these. When the radar transmits its signal to the beacon, it is said to *interrogate* or *ask a question*. If the beacon receives the correct code, it *responds*. The beacon is also called a *transponder*.

A typical application of a beacon is the *IFF radar*. The initials stand for *I*nformation *F*riend or *F*oe. During airplane battles, ground anti-aircraft batteries can detect the planes with radar but cannot distinguish between friendly and enemy planes. To prevent shooting down friendly planes, these planes carry IFF radars. The ground stations interrogate the beacons and if the beacon responds, the plane is known to be friendly; otherwise, it is shot down.

Beacons may also be used on weather satellites. As the satellite circumnavigates the earth, its sensors gather weather data. When the satellite is overhead, its beacon is interrogated, and it transmits the weather information back to the ground station.

6-11 SEA SURVEILLANCE

Similar to the air-traffic control problem is the problem of avoiding collisions of ships on the sea and in harbors. To avoid collisions on the sea, ships usually carry a radar on top of a mast. In harbors, a land-based radar is used. Whether the radar is on the ship or on land, the targets are all at sea level, and it is thus not necessary to search in elevation. The radar used is similar to the radar which monitors surface traffic at airports. It uses a fan beam with a cosecant-squared pattern, high repetition rate, and narrow pulses.

PROBLEMS

6-1. What is the difference between a search radar and a tracking radar?

6-2. List four target properties which can be measured by a tracking radar.

6-3. Describe two types of antenna beams which could be used with a search radar. What are the advantages of each type?

6-4. Sketch the error signal (as a function of time) of a conical scanning radar for (a) a large error, (b) a small error, and (c) no error.

6-5. What is the major difference between a sequential lobing tracking radar and an amplitude monopulse tracking radar?

6-6. What is the advantage of a track-while-scan radar when compared to a continuous tracker?

6-7. A particular Doppler navigator which operates at a frequency of 10 000 MHz measures a Doppler frequency of 4000 Hz. If its antenna is mounted at an angle of 60° from the direction of flight ($\theta = 60°$), what is the aircraft velocity?

ans: 400 ft/second

6-8. What information must a fire control radar provide to a computer for accurate aiming of guns?

6-9. What is the function of early warning radar systems? Describe their major characteristics.

6-10. How do airport ground-traffic monitor radars and air-traffic control radars differ in antenna beam, pulse repetition frequency, and pulse duration?

6-11. What are the major considerations in choosing an operating frequency for a weather-avoidance radar?

6-12. What is the function of an IFF radar system?

6-13. An airborne interceptor radar which has a 1° pencil beam is required to search a volume in space which is 10° by 10°. Its pulse repetition frequency is 2000 pps, and 100 pulses must be received from a target for detection. What is the minimum time in which the volume can be searched?   *ans:*   5 seconds

CHAPTER SEVEN

Reception and Noise

7-1 THE NATURE OF NOISE

Electrons in motion generate electric currents which have the appearance of random signals. In any practical receiver, electrons are in constant motion, and, therefore, the receiver will always have a measurable voltage at the output which depends upon the motion of the electrons. The electrons may move in conductors or in interelectrode gaps, but in either case unwanted "signals" are created. Since these signals are random in both amplitude and frequency, they are called *noise*, and their power level is called *noise power*.

The motion of electrons in a conductor or resistance is dependent on the temperature. The maximum noise power that can be transferred to the load from this source is

$$\text{N.P.} = KTB \qquad (7\text{-}1)$$

where N.P. is noise power

K is Boltzmann's constant $= 1.38 \times 10^{-23}$ joule per degree

T is temperature in degrees Kelvin

B is bandwidth over which the noise is measured

Since the noise from this source is proportional to temperature, it is known as *thermal noise*. It is independent of frequency and occurs in all the radar bands. This is the main source of noise.

In electronic devices, electrons are emitted from a cathode randomly. Although the average motion of the electrons is constant, the individual electrons arrive at the anode at random times and thus cause random noise currents. This is called *shot noise*.

In semiconductor devices at low frequencies, there is a source of noise due to the irregular motion of electrons. This noise is inversely proportional to the frequency and becomes negligible above about 100 kHz. It was described in Sec. 4-6 and is called *one-over-f* $(1/f)$ *noise.*

7-2 SENSITIVITY

If receivers added no noise to incoming signals, any signal could be detected, no matter how weak. However, the noise generated in a practical receiver will mask a weak signal so that it cannot be detected. An amplifier in the receiver which increases the signal level also increases the noise level. The *sensitivity* of a receiver is simply the strength of the weakest input signal which will produce a specified level at the output terminals or on the display.

As indicated in Sec. 1-7, there are two general types of radar receivers, the video receiver and the superheterodyne. There are two different output specifications to express the sensitivity of a video receiver: *minimum detectable signal* (MDS), and *tangential sensitivity* (TS). Both are expressed in decibels below a milliwatt or −dbm. Thus a signal strength of 1 microwatt is 30 db below a milliwatt, or simply −30 dbm.

The minimum detectable signal or MDS is, as its name implies, the strength of the weakest signal which can be detected. Unfortunately, this is not a reliable specification, since it depends to a large extent on the experience.

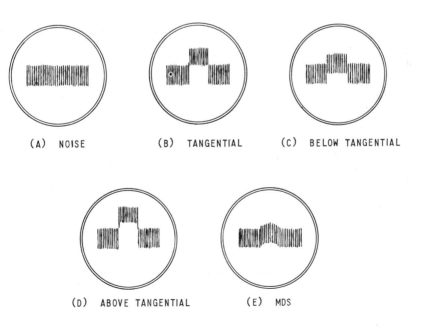

　　(A) NOISE　　　　　　(B) TANGENTIAL　　　　(C) BELOW TANGENTIAL

　　　　(D) ABOVE TANGENTIAL　　　　(E) MDS

Fig. 7-1. Sensitivity displays.

of the operator and the type of presentation (visual or aural). The ability to pick out a signal from the background noise improves with experience.

Tangential sensitivity is a more reliable measure, since different operators will obtain consistent measurements of this quantity. The term applies to the power of a signal which is just equal to the background noise, that is, the signal-to-noise ratio is unity. The types of presentations seen on the display are shown in Fig. 7-1. In Fig. 7-1(a), only the background noise is shown. Fig. 7-1(b) shows a signal which raises a portion of the noise line so that its bottom is just tangent to the top of the rest of the noise. This is *tangential sensitivity*. The signal level is thus just equal to the noise level. The strength of the signal at the input to the receiver is, then, the sensitivity of the receiver on the basis of tangential sensitivity. This is not, however, the weakest signal that can be detected. Figure 7-1(c) shows a weaker signal and Fig. 7-1(d) shows a stronger signal than is shown in Fig. 7-1(b).

In Fig. 7-1(e), a signal is just beginning. This may be MDS for some operators while others may not notice it. The minimum detectable signal is obviously weaker than the value determined as the tangential sensitivity of the receiver. As a rule of thumb, it is generally assumed that an average operator can spot a signal about 4 db weaker than the value of the tangential sensitivity.

The sensitivity of a video receiver varies inversely as the square root of the bandwidth. That is, if the bandwidth is increased by a factor of 4, the sensitivity will be decreased by a factor of 2 (3 dbm). For example, if a video receiver has a sensitivity of -55 dbm with a 1-MHz bandwidth amplifier, it will have a sensitivity of -52 dbm with a 4-MHz bandwidth amplifier.

The sensitivity of a superheterodyne receiver or of a mixer is defined as the signal power which is 3 db more than the noise power. Since noise power varies with temperature, as indicated in Eq. (7-1), a standard temperature must be assumed. The standard temperature agreed upon is 290°K (about room temperature), and at this value, the sensitivity of a superheterodyne receiver is

$$S_{db} = -171 \text{ dbm} + 10 \log B + F_{db} \tag{7-2}$$

where S_{db} is the sensitivity in dbm

B is the bandwidth in Hz

F_{db} is the noise figure of the receiver in decibels

Thus, if the receiver has a bandwidth of 2 MHz and a noise figure of 20 db, then $10 \log B = 63$, and

$$S_{db} = -171 + 63 + 20 = -88 \text{ dbm} \tag{7-3}$$

The term *noise figure* is a measure of the noise generated in the receiver and will be explained in the next section. It should be noted that the sensitivity in a superheterodyne is inversely proportional to the bandwidth, rather than the square root of the bandwidth as in a video receiver.

Since in both types of receivers the sensitivity decreases with increased bandwidth, it seems logical to make the bandwidth as narrow as possible. However, the video amplifier bandwidth must be wide enough to pass the frequencies in the pulse envelope. For good pulse reproduction, the bandwidth of the video amplifier should be on the order of the reciprocal of the pulse width. That is,

$$\tau B = 1 \tag{7-4}$$

Thus, to reproduce a 1-μsec pulse ($\tau = 10^{-6}$), the bandwidth should be about 1 MHz ($1.0/10^{-6}$). There is experimental evidence that 1.2 times this value is optimum, but the variation with bandwidth near this value is small, so that any value between 1 and 2 may be used.

7-3 NOISE FIGURE

From Eq. (7-2) it is evident that the higher the noise figure, the lower the sensitivity, and, in fact, when the bandwidth of a receiver is specified, the noise figure is the factor which limits sensitivity. Noise figure is a measure of the noise generated in the circuits of the network or receiver. There is always some noise at the input, designated N_i. The input signal is designated S_i and, therefore, the *signal-to-noise ratio* at the input is S_i/N_i. At the output, the signal will be changed by the gain of the network or receiver to S_o. (The gain can be negative as well as positive.) The input noise is also modified in the same manner by the gain. The output noise, N_o, is the sum of this modified input noise plus the noise generated in the receiver. The output signal-to-noise ratio is S_o/N_o. The noise factor is the ratio of the input signal-to-noise to the output signal-to-noise; thus:

$$F = \frac{S_i}{N_i} \div \frac{S_o}{N_o} \tag{7-5}$$

or

$$F = \frac{S_i N_o}{N_i S_o}$$

If there were no noise generated in the receiver, the input signal-to-noise ratio would be the same as the output signal-to-noise ratio, and F would be unity. The *noise figure*, F_{db}, is simply the noise factor expressed in decibels:

$$F_{db} = 10 \log F = 10 \log \frac{S_i/N_i}{S_o/N_o} \tag{7-6}$$

A perfect receiver, then, would have a noise figure of 0 db.

7-4 EFFECT OF RF AMPLIFIER

If an RF amplifier is placed in front of a receiver, both the incoming signal and the noise will be amplified. However, if the amplifier has a low noise figure, it is possible that the ratio of amplified signal to the sum of the amplifier output noise and receiver input noise will be greater than the input signal-to-noise ratio at the receiver without the amplifier. The net result would be a reduction in the overall noise figure and thus an increase in sensitivity.

When two networks are connected in series, the overall *noise factor* is

$$F_T = F_1 + \frac{F_2 - 1}{G_1} \qquad (7\text{-}7)$$

where F_T is the total or overall noise factor

F_1 is the noise factor of the first or input network

F_2 is the noise factor of the second network

G_1 is the gain of the first network

For example, assume a receiver has a noise figure of 14 db; its noise factor is 25. Suppose an amplifier with a gain of 13 db and noise figure of 3 db is placed ahead of it. Then

$$F_1 = 2 \qquad (10 \log 2 = 3)$$
$$F_2 = 25 \qquad (10 \log 25 = 14)$$
$$G_1 = 20 \qquad (10 \log 20 = 13)$$

From Eq. (7-7)

$$F_T = 2 + \frac{24}{20} = 3.2 \qquad (7\text{-}8)$$

This is a noise figure of about 5 db, or about 9 db better sensitivity than without the amplifier.

If a second stage of amplification is added, Eq. (7-7) can be used again to calculate the overall noise figure. Suppose the second amplifier has the same values as the first. The values of $F_T = 3.2$ given by Eq. (7-8) is now the value of the new F_2, that is, the receiver and first amplifier together make up a single box. Then, from Eq. (7-7)

$$F_T = 2 + \frac{2.2}{20} = 2.11 \quad \text{or about 3.2 db}$$

This is only 1.8 db better and may not be worth the additional cost and complexity.

7-5 PROBABILITY OF DETECTION

The designer of a radar receiver is concerned with noise figure and mini-mum detectable signal as described earlier in this chapter. However, the designer of a radar system is concerned with probability of detection of a target, rather than the detection of a single echo. The noise in a receiver has a random fluctuation, and at times some of the noise peaks will look like signals. Since observed signal levels are really the sum of signal and noise components, weak signals also look like noise.

An experienced operator will see more targets than an inexperienced one and is less likely to be fooled into mistaking noise for a target. However, to evaluate a radar, a standard operator must be assumed. To do this, a signal threshold level is set in the receiver. All signals above this threshold are assumed to be received, and all below are missed. Any noise peak which exceeds the threshold appears as a signal and is called a *false alarm*. A certain number of false alarms are permissible. The threshold must be set to detect as many echoes as possible without making the number of false alarms excessive.

If a receiver is shut off part of the time, the chance of a noise peak exceeding the threshold is reduced. That is, the probability that a noise peak will appear as a false alarm applies continuously, and if some of the noise peaks are removed by turning off the receiver, some false alarms must be removed also. This is why the use of range gates in a receiver, as described in Sec. 5-7, reduces the average probability of false alarms.

Integration of pulses, as described in Sec. 3-9, increases the signal-to-noise ratio of a target signal. Thus, the threshold can be set at a higher level than would be required for detection of a single echo, and in this way the probability of false alarms is lowered.

7-6 MATCHED FILTER

It is possible to improve the signal-to-noise output of a receiver by using a *matched filter*. A matched filter is simply a network designed to maximize the signal-to-noise ratio of the particular signals desired. For example, if the received signal were a pure sine wave, the matched filter could be approxi-mated by a simple high-Q, resonant circuit tuned to the frequency of the signal. Since this is a narrow-band network, it would reduce noise, which is proportional to bandwidth.

In practice, of course, most radar signals are not sine waves, but pulses which are usually rectangular, but may be any shape. If the echoes are simple rectangular pulses, it is possible to build a matched filter which will maximize reception of pulses of the specific pulse length being used. Pulses of other durations, and thus random noise pulses, will be attenuated through the filter. In this way, the filter acts to improve the output signal-to-noise ratio and to reduce false alarms.

If returned echoes always have the same characteristics, a matched filter could be designed to optimize reception of that characteristic. However, if different types of transmitted pulses are used at different times, a simple matched filter would not optimize every received signal and, in fact, might degrade some pulse shapes. One implementation of a matched filter receiver which compares the received echo to the transmitted signal is called a cross-correlation receiver. Its operation is indicated in Fig. 7-2. A pulse is transmitted, starting at time $t = 0$. A small part of the transmitted pulse, with shape and duration preserved, is delayed a time t_s and then fed into the mixer. For the pictured delay time, the pulse is shown occurring from $t = A$ to $t = B$. A received pulse of the same shape is also applied to the mixer and is shown occurring from $t = C$ to $t = D$. In the mixer, the two pulses are multiplied. Since the delayed pulse is zero beyond B and the received echo is zero before C, the only output of the multiplication will occur between $t = C$ and $t = B$. If the delay t_s were exactly correct, the two pulses would coincide and the product would be a maximum. The output of the detector is applied to a filter which rejects all products below a predetermined threshold. In practice, the delay time t_s may be varied, and when the output is maximum, the corresponding delay time also indicates the range of the target. If a noise pulse occurs, even at the same point in time as the delayed pulse, it will not cause a false alarm unless it also satisfies the unlikely condition that it resemble the transmitted pulse.

The shape of the transmitted pulse need not be rectangular. Since the shape of the received pulse is similar to that of the transmitted pulse (except as affected by target motion), it may be easier to build a matched filter for a shape other than rectangular.

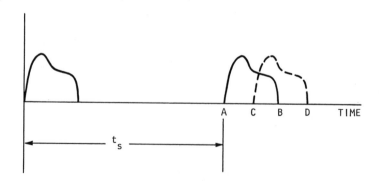

Fig. 7-2. Cross-correlation.

7-7 PULSE COMPRESSION

The velocity of propagation of electromagnetic energy in free space is approximately 1000 ft per microsecond. If the difference in range between two targets is 1000 ft and they are illuminated in range by a 2-μsec pulse, the echo from the first would end just as the echo from the second began. If they were closer, it would be impossible to resolve the two echoes with a 2-μsec pulse. Range resolution is dependent on the pulse width. If the pulse could be compressed on reception, it would be possible to improve range resolution.

One form of pulse compression is achieved by frequency-modulating the transmitted pulse. Assume the transmitted pulse is 2 μsec long and increases in frequency linearly from f_1 at the start to f_2 2 μsec later. The echo also has this characteristic. The matched filter in the receiver is a pulse compression filter in which the velocity of propagation depends on the frequency. The lower frequencies at the start of the pulse are slowed with respect to the higher frequencies at the end of the pulse. If the frequency-dependence is linear, the output of the pulse compression filter is a much shorter pulse of increased amplitude. The *compression ratio* is

$$\text{C.R.} = (f_2 - f_1)\tau \qquad (7\text{-}9)$$

In practice, a compression ratio of 100 to 1 is readily achievable, so that the 2-μsec pulse could be compressed to one-hundredth of its width or 20 nanoseconds, corresponding to a range resolution of 10 ft. Compression ratios as high as 1000 have been reported.

The frequency modulation need not be linear. It is only necessary that the pulse compression filter matches the transmitted pulse in frequency characteristics. This type of pulse compression is sometimes called *chirp*.

PROBLEMS

7-1. List three types of noise which affect reception. Which type has the least effect upon typical radar receivers? Why?

7-2. What is the thermal noise power at the output of a 1 MHz filter which is at room temperature (290°K)? Express your answer in watts and in units of dbm.
ans. 4×10^{-15} watts, -114 dbm

7-3. Explain the difference between minimum detectable signal and tangential sensitivity.

7-4. How is sensitivity defined for a superheterodyne receiver? Compare this definition to that of tangential sensitivity for a video receiver.

7-5. Discuss the trade-offs involved in the choice of bandwidth for a video amplifier. What bandwidth should be used in a system with a 4-μsec pulse?

ans: between 250 kHz and 500 kHz

7-6.   What is the noise factor and noise figure of a network which has an output signal-to-noise ratio of 2.5 when the input signal-to-noise ratio is 10?

ans: 4, 6 db

7-7.   What is the sensitivity of the superheterodyne receiver in Prob. 7-6 if it is designed for a 5-μsec pulse (using the $2/\tau$ design rule)?   *ans:* -109 dbm

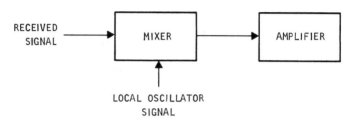

Fig. P-7-8.   Superheterodyne receiver.

7-8.   A typical superheterodyne receiver which does not have an RF amplifier is shown in Fig. P-7-8. The mixer has a conversion loss of 3 db (i.e., a gain of $\frac{1}{2}$) and a noise figure of 10 db. The amplifier has a noise figure of 6 db. What is the overall noise figure?   *ans:*   12 db

7-9.   If an RF amplifier with a gain of 13 db and a noise figure of 3 db is placed in front of the receiver of Fig. P-7-8, what is the overall noise factor? What is the noise figure?   *ans:*   2.75, 4.4 db

7-10.   What is a false alarm? How can a radar operator change the false alarm probability?

7-11.   What advantage do range gates provide with regard to false alarms?

7-12.   What is the major property of a matched filter?

7-13.   Describe the operation of a cross-correlation receiver.

7-14.   A chirp signal is produced by linearly modulating a 1-μsec pulse from 9700 MHz to 9900 MHz. What is the compression rate? What is the range resolution?

ans: 200, 2.5 ft

7-15.   Prove the important fact that range resolution of a chirp radar is given by

$$\frac{c}{2(f_2 - f_1)}$$

where c is the speed of light. (*Hint:* Compute the duration of the compressed pulse and then use the relationship that the range resolution is $c\tau/2$.)

CHAPTER EIGHT

Propagation

8-1 LINE-OF-SIGHT

Microwave signals and light waves are both electromagnetic waves and thus have similar properties. Like light, microwaves travel in straight lines. This implies that a target can only be detected if it is in line-of-sight. That is, it will not be visible if it is below the horizon. However, again like light waves, microwaves are affected by refraction, reflection, and divergence, which change the path of propagation. These effects will be explained in the following sections.

8-2 REFLECTION

If both the radar and the target are near the earth so that the earth itself is within the antenna beamwidth, then, beside the direct wave from the antenna to the target, there will be a wave reflected from the earth. If the two waves are in phase when they reach the target, in effect, an increased signal arrives there and, of course, a stronger echo is received. Thus, the range of the radar is increased for targets which are favorably situated. If the two waves are out of phase, they will cancel, producing a reduced signal at the target and a reduced echo. In this case, the radar could be ineffective even for a relatively close target.

Figure 8-1 illustrates the geometry of the waves, assuming that the earth is a plane surface. A radar antenna is located at point A at a height h_1 above the earth. The target (for example, a plane) is at T at a height h_2 above the earth and a ground distance R from the radar antenna. The direct ray is the line AT. The reflected ray from A hits the earth at E and is reflected to T. The angle β is the angle that the incident and reflected parts of the reflected wave

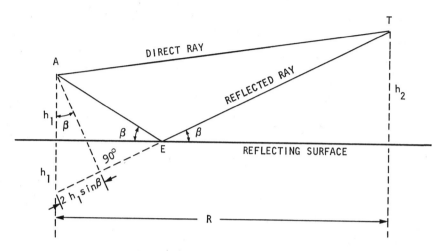

Fig. 8-1. Reflection from flat earth.

make with the earth. From simple trigonometry, assuming R is large compared to h_1 and h_2, the difference in path length between the direct and reflected waves is

$$\Delta L = 2h_1 \sin \beta \qquad (8\text{-}1)$$

The ground range is given by

$$R = \frac{h_1}{\tan \beta} + \frac{h_2}{\tan \beta} = \frac{h_1 + h_2}{\tan \beta} \qquad (8\text{-}2)$$

Since β is very small for large R, $\sin \beta = \tan \beta$. Then from Eqs. (8-1) and (8-2)

$$\Delta L = \frac{2h_1(h_1 + h_2)}{R} \qquad (8\text{-}3)$$

Usually the radar is located on a structure on the earth, and the target is a plane. In this case, h_2 is much larger than h_1 so that Eq. (8-3) becomes approximately

$$\Delta L = \frac{2h_1 h_2}{R} \qquad (8\text{-}4)$$

The phase difference corresponding to this path-length difference is

$$\Delta \phi = \frac{2\pi}{\lambda} \cdot \frac{2h_1 h_2}{R} = \frac{4\pi h_1 h_2}{\lambda R} \text{ radians} \qquad (8\text{-}5)$$

If the total phase difference, $\Delta \phi$, is equal to an even multiple of π, the two waves are in phase, and a signal maximum results. That is, for a maximum,

$$\frac{4h_1h_2}{\lambda R} = 2n \tag{8-6}$$

For a minimum, $\Delta\phi$ must be an odd multiple of π. That is, for a minimum or null,

$$\frac{4h_1h_2}{\lambda R} = 2n + 1 \tag{8-7}$$

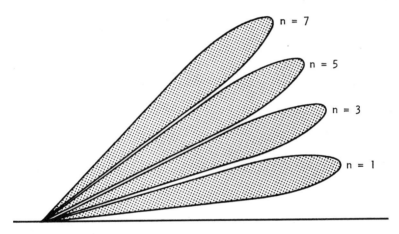

Fig. 8-2. Lobe structure.

The resultant antenna pattern is a lobe arrangement as shown in Fig. 8-2.

Equations (8-6) and (8-7), however, do not take into consideration any phase change or amplitude change which occurs at the reflecting surface of the earth. These will be considered in Sec. 8-4.

8-3 DIVERGENCE

The curvature of the earth causes divergence or spreading of the rays of a signal reflected from its surface. This is shown in Fig. 8-3. The bundle of incident rays are shown as parallel, but after reflection, the rays diverge, so that the total energy arriving at a target is decreased.

In calculating a radiation pattern which involves reflections from earth, the effects of divergence are included by multiplying the pattern by a *divergence factor*. This is zero at grazing incidence and unity at normal incidence. For most practical angles a value of 0.5 may be assumed, which causes a smoothing of the pattern, as indicated in the next section.

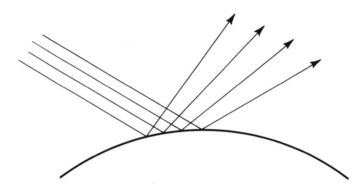

Fig. 8-3.   Divergence.

8-4 REFLECTION COEFFICIENTS

In the derivation in Sec. 8-2, it was assumed that there was perfect reflection from the earth without change of phase. However, in the actual case, the reflection is affected by the nature of the surface of the earth and by the polarity of the microwave signal. If the earth were a perfect reflecting surface, the reflection coefficient would be unity without change of phase for vertically polarized signals and would be unity with a phase change of π radians for horizontally polarized signals. For a less than perfect reflecting conductor such as the surface of the sea, the horizontally polarized signal still has a phase change of π radians, but the vertically polarized signal's phase is a function of both frequency and angle of incidence. At small angles at microwave frequencies, it also approaches π radians. Thus, for the real environment, Eqs. (8-6) and (8-7) should be interchanged. Equation (8-6) is the equation for minima and Eq. (8-7) is the equation for maxima, when the reflection coefficient of -1 is taken into consideration.

The *amplitude* of the reflection coefficient is unity if the surface is a perfect reflector. In practice, however, the surface is rough and not a good conductor, so that some energy is lost by scattering and some by absorption. The results of the imperfect reflection are smaller maxima and shallower nulls in the lobe pattern of Fig. 8-2. The effects of divergence cause further "smoothing" of the pattern. Nevertheless, the lobe structure of the pattern is observable. As a moving target, such as a plane, passes through the lobes, the echoes are alternately stronger and weaker. In general, the lobing due to reflection causes enhancement of the signal when the target is favorably situated. The net result is that a plane will be picked up at greater ranges as it passes through a lobe maximum, but it will not be detected continuously as it approaches.

8-5 REFRACTION

Radar waves travel in straight lines in free space, but close to the earth they are refracted or bent by the varying density of the atmosphere. Thus, a target will appear displaced from its true position. Corrections must be applied to measurements of vertical displacement to account for the effect of refraction. This is especially true in height-finding or altitude radars.

Another effect of refraction is that signals will be bent so that targets below the horizon can be detected. Thus, the radar apparently sees targets which are below the line of sight.

It is possible to correct for both effects by assuming that the earth is larger than it is and that the earth's atmosphere varies uniformly. *Standard refraction* is the refraction which assumes an atmosphere in which signals travel in straight lines and that the earth's radius is multiplied by $\frac{4}{3}$. This model of the enlarged earth comes close to producing theoretical horizons which agree with observations.

The distance from a radar at height h to the horizon may be determined by simple geometry. The radius of the earth is approximately 3450 n.mi. For radar, the earth is assumed to be $\frac{4}{3}$ as large, or the radius of the "radar" earth is 4600 n.mi. On this earth, the distance to the *radar horizon* is

$$d = 1.23 \sqrt{h_1} \tag{8-8}$$

where d is in nautical miles

h_1 is in feet

The distance computed from Eq. (8-8) agrees with observations. It is approximately 16 percent more than the distance to the true, or optical, horizon. If the target is at a height h_2, the maximum range at which it can be detected is

$$R_{max} = 1.23 \sqrt{h_1} + 1.23 \sqrt{h_2} = 1.23(\sqrt{h_1} + \sqrt{h_2}) \tag{8-9}$$

8-6 ANOMALOUS PROPAGATION

It is possible for a layer of warm air to occur above a layer of cool air in the atmosphere, contrary to the normal temperature gradient. This is called a *temperature inversion*. The resultant change in the index of refraction may cause signals to follow the curvature of the earth. The phenomenon is called superrefraction or anomalous propagation, and the signals travel in apparent ducts for tremendous distances, far beyond the radar horizon.

8-7 ATTENUATION

The atmosphere of the earth contains many gases which absorb radar signals in varying amounts, but only oxygen and water vapor produce significant attenuation. Energy absorbed by these two gases is converted to heat and is lost.

The one-way absorption due to water vapor varies with frequency. At 2 GHz, it is about 0.0002 db per nautical mile, and it increases to a peak of about 0.2 db per nautical mile at about 22 GHz. Absorption due to oxygen is almost constant at 0.02 db per nautical mile at microwave frequencies up to about 20 GHz. It then rises sharply to a peak of about 0 db per nautical mile at 60 GHz. Other peaks occur at about 180 GHz for water vapor and 120 GHz for oxygen.

The attenuation caused by oxygen and water vapor appears as a reduction in range for the radar. When calculating the loss factor L in Eq. (3-14) in Sec. 3-10, this two-way loss must be included.

8-8 PRECIPITATION

Rain, snow, fog, and hail have two important effects on radar signals. In the first place, they reflect signals, in effect, acting as radar targets. Thus, less energy is available for observing desired targets. The unwanted echoes from precipitation are called *meteorological echoes* or *weather clutter*. It is possible to minimize these reflections by proper choice of frequencies as was explained in Sec. 3-2. If the purpose of the radar is to detect precipitation, then reflections would be maximized by choice of frequency.

A second effect of precipitation is attenuation due to absorption. The attenuation has been found empirically to be approximately

$$\alpha = \frac{M}{\lambda^2} \tag{8-10}$$

where α = attenuation in db per nautical mile

  M = moisture in grams per cubic meter

  λ = wavelength of transmitted signal in centimeters

The effect of precipitation attenuation is to reduce range in exactly the same manner that atmospheric attenuation does. It also should be included in the loss factor L in Eq. (3-14).

PROBLEMS

8-1. Explain how the existence of both direct waves and reflected waves at a target can affect radar performance.

8-2. A radar located 30 ft above the earth's surface observes an aircraft at a range of 10 n.mi. (60 000 ft) and an altitude of 2500 ft. Assuming no amplitude or phase change upon reflection, will the signal be maximum or minimum if the radar wavelength is 0.1 ft? 0.2 ft? What is n in each case?   *ans:*   25, 12

8-3.   A target at a range of 100 000 ft and an altitude of 10 000 ft produces a maximum return for a radar 20 ft above the ground operating with a wavelength of 1 ft. By how much must the range decrease for the target to produce a minimum if the altitude is held constant?   *ans:*   11 000 ft

8-4.   How does di. .gence of the radiated energy affect radar performance?

8-5.   At microwave frequencies, by about what amount is the phase of a reflected signal changed? How is the amplitude of a reflected wave altered?

8-6.   Discuss qualitatively how Fig. 8-2 would look for an actual situation involving imperfect reflection.

8-7.   Explain the difference between reflection and refraction.

8-8.   List two ways in which refraction affects radar performance.

8-9.   How far away is the radar horizon for an airborne radar at an altitude of 10 000 ft? How far away is the optical horizon at this altitude?

ans: 123 n.mi., 106 n.mi.

8-10.   How do temperature inversion layers affect long distance radar propagation?

8-11.   How much loss due to water vapor and oxygen will a 2 GHz radar experience when observing a target at a range of 20 n.mi.? What is the approximate loss if the radar operates at 22 GHz?   *ans:*   0.808 db, 8.8 db

8-12.   How does attenuation by atmospheric gases affect radar performance?

8-13.   List two effects that precipitation has upon radar signals.

8-14.   Approximately, how does attenuation caused by precipitation vary with frequency? What is the ratio of attenuation at 10 GHz to that at 1 GHz?

CHAPTER NINE

Radar Systems Design

9-1 ANALYSIS AND SYNTHESIS

When a company decides to market a new bottled drink, or a new gadget for a car, or any other item sold to the consumer, the most important question is, "Will it sell?" The new product must fill a need, or the company must feel that it can create the desire to buy by suitable advertising. The design of a radar system is quite different in that a company never builds a new radar system first and then tries to sell it. Instead, a new requirement is created by new technology, such as advanced weapon development or space observation. Or perhaps a new scientific breakthrough permits building a better radar to meet a hitherto unsatisfied requirement. The design of a new radar system, then, usually begins with a requirement or a set of specifications.

The process of designing a radar system begins with an analysis of the requirements. What does it have to do? What is the environment in which it must work? Environment includes other electromagnetic signals which may accidentally or purposely interfere with the operation of the radar, as well as climate and geography. After the problem has been analyzed, the systems engineer considers the possible solutions. This may require development of new components or circuits, or it may be possible to build a suitable system with existing parts. There may be several possible solutions, each with its own advantages and limitations. It is then necessary for the systems engineer to weigh each against the others and choose the best for the job. For example, if a system can be built with existing parts, but a better one can be built after further development, the engineer must decide whether the advantages gained by the second are worth the extra cost and time necessary.

The process of analyzing the problem is called *systems analysis*. After analyzing the problem, the system parameters are specified. Now the system is built and tested. This process is called *systems synthesis*. Synthesis is the opposite of analysis. In analysis, a system is given and the engineer determines what it will do, whereas in synthesis, the performance is given, and the engineer determines the system which will have the required performance.

9-2 SPECIFICATIONS

After the requirements are determined and a system selected, the specifications of the system must be determined. The important parameters to be specified are:

Frequency, f, or wavelength, λ

Peak power, P_p

Pulse width, τ

Pulse repetition rate, f_r

Receiver sensitivity or other receiver characteristics, S_{min}

Antenna beamwidth, BW

Antenna scan rate, ω_s

Antenna gain, G, or effective area, A_e

System losses, L

The methods of determining these quantities make use of the equations discussed thus far in the text. The techniques will be illustrated by an example, the design of a shipborne radar to detect military aircraft at sea.

9-3 REQUIREMENTS

It is required to detect approaching planes at altitudes up to 10 000 ft as early as possible and to track these planes to within 12 miles of the ship. The radar antenna is to be located on a point on the ship 100 ft above the surface of the sea.

First the *maximum range* must be determined. From Eq. (8-9),

$$R_{\max} = 1.23(\sqrt{h_1} + \sqrt{h_2})$$
$$R_{\max} = 1.23(\sqrt{100} + \sqrt{10\ 000}) = 135.3 \text{ n.mi.} \tag{9-1}$$

If a plane is at 10 000 ft, it will be detectable at about 135 n.mi., but if it flies close to the surface, it will be below the horizon until it is $1.23\sqrt{100} = 12.3$ n.mi. away (almost the minimum range).

Since the radar must see all planes up to 12 miles away, its vertical coverage must be the angle made by 10 000 ft and 12 n.mi., as indicated in Fig. 9-1.

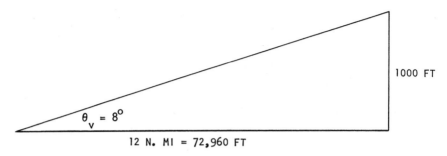

Fig. 9-1. Vertical beamwidth.

$$\tan \theta_v = \frac{10\,000}{72\,960} = 0.137$$

$$\theta_v \approx 8°$$

In azimuth the antenna must scan through 360°, since the plane can approach from any direction.

Of course, planes higher than 10 000 ft will be visible at the maximum range and will remain visible until the elevation angle, with respect to the radar antenna, exceeds $\theta_v = 8°$. Thus, a plane at 30 000 ft, for example, will have an elevation angle of 8° at three times the range of a plane at 10 000 ft. That is, it will be visible until it is about 36 n.mi. from the radar antenna.

Since multiple targets may occur, track-while-scan is specified as a requirement. This permits tracking several planes while searching for others, as was explained in Sec. 6-4. It is also required that the range resolution be $\frac{1}{2}$ n.mi.

Since there is no ground clutter at sea, it is unnecessary to use MTI or other Doppler discriminating radar.

9-4 ANTENNA SPECIFICATIONS

From the previously calculated requirements, the antenna beam must sweep through 360° in azimuth and 8° in elevation. This can be accomplished by the use of a fan beam which covers 8° vertically and sweeps through 360° in azimuth. It will be assumed that a height-finder antenna is also used, but the details of that will not be included in this example. The azimuth beamwidth is a compromise among several factors. A narrow beam is more accurate but requires a larger antenna. Also, since the beam is on the target a shorter period of time in each scan, there are fewer pulses to integrate and, thus, more power is required. As an arbitrary compromise, it will be assumed that a 2° azimuth beamwidth is satisfactory.

The antenna size depends on the frequency, as given by Eq. (2-6).

$$\text{BW} = \frac{70\lambda}{D} \tag{9-2}$$

This is the equation for a parabolic antenna with tapered illumination, where λ is the wavelength and D the aperture. Table 9-1 shows D, the aperture, for three different values of λ.

TABLE 9-1

	X-BAND	C-BAND	S-BAND
Approximate f	10 000 MHz	5000 MHz	3000 MHz
λ	0.098 ft	0.197 ft	0.328 ft
D for 2° BW	3.4 ft	6.9 ft	11.5 ft
D for 8° BW	0.86 ft	1.72 ft	2.87 ft
Antenna size	3.4 ft × 0.86 ft	6.9 ft × 1.72 ft	11.5 ft × 2.87 ft
Approximate A_e	1.5 ft²	6 ft²	16.5 ft²

The effective area, A_e, of the antenna is approximately half the true area for a parabolic section with tapered illumination. The values shown in the table may be off as much as 10 percent, but, as will be shown, overall accuracies are no better than this.

The three sizes of antenna are all feasible. The choice of frequency, then, will depend on other requirements and specifications. This is discussed in the next section.

9-5 FREQUENCY

Components and power tubes exist for all three frequencies, so any would be a possible choice. However, as was discussed in Sec. 8-7, the attenuation due to oxygen and water vapor in the atmosphere increases with frequency in this range. Another consideration is absorption and reflection caused by rain, since the radar should operate successfully in all weather. The attenuation caused by absorption is given by Eq. (8-10).

$$\alpha = \frac{M}{\lambda^2} \tag{9-3}$$

Here again, the attenuation is lower when the wavelength is larger, that is, at lower frequencies. Reflection from raindrops is a function of frequency, as explained in Sec. 3-2. To minimize reflections, the wavelength should be large compared to the circumference of the drops. In this respect, too, the

S-band frequencies are preferable. In fact, as was explained in Sec. 6-9, X-band and C-band are usually chosen for weather radars because reflections from raindrops are enhanced at these frequencies.

Thus an S-band radar will be used and the antenna will be about $11\frac{1}{2}$ ft by $2\frac{7}{8}$ ft. The antenna will be mounted with its long direction horizontal so that the beam is narrow in azimuth and wide in elevation.

9-6 PULSE PARAMETERS

The pulse width is limited by the required range resolution of half a mile. From Sec. 3-4, the time for a signal to travel half a mile and return is half of 12.4 μsec or 6.2 μsec. This is the maximum pulse width. Thus, a pulse 6 μsec wide will be selected.

The inter-pulse interval is determined by the maximum range, in this case about 135 n.mi. Again, allowing 12.4 μsec per mile, the pulse interval should be at least $12.4 \times 135 = 1674$ μsec. From Eq. (1.1), which relates pulse interval to repetition frequency:

$$\text{pulse interval} = \frac{1}{f_r} \qquad (9\text{-}4)$$

the pulse repetition frequency is $10^6/1674 = 597$. To permit duplexer circuits and sweep circuits to recover, f_r will be chosen as 500.

The duty cycle, as discussed in Sec. 1-3, is the product of pulse width, τ, and repetition frequency, f_r. In this radar, then, the duty cycle is $6 \times 10^{-6} \times 500 = 0.003$.

Pulse compression is not necessary for range resolution, but it may be required to put a large burst of power on the target because of excessive range.

9-7 RECEIVER SENSITIVITY

The sensitivity of a superheterodyne receiver at about room temperature is given by Eq. (7-2).

$$S_{\text{db}} = -171 \text{ dbm} + 10 \log B + F_{\text{db}} \qquad (9\text{-}5)$$

The bandwidth B is related to the pulse width τ by Eq. (7-4).

$$\tau B = 1 \qquad (9\text{-}6)$$

In this case $\tau = 6$ μsec. Therefore $B = 167$ kHz. Then in Eq. (9-5), 10 $\log B = 10 \log 167\,000 = 42$ db. The value of F_{db} depends on the state of the art. A noise figure of 10 db at S-band is easily achievable. Thus,

$S_{db} = -171 + 42 + 10 = -119$ dbm $= 1.2 \times 10^{-15}$ watts. This value will be used for S_{min} in the radar equation.

9-8 LOSSES

Section 3-10 indicated many sources of loss in a radar system. These include RF loss, mismatch loss, beam-shape loss, collapsing loss, operator loss, and propagation loss. Values of propagation loss were indicated in Sec. 8-7. The two-way propagation loss due to oxygen is 0.04 db per nautical mile or, in this case, $0.04 \times 135 = 5.4$ db. The water vapor loss is negligible at S-band. The other system losses may amount to 8 to 10 db. Assume a total, including propagation loss, of 15 db or 31.6 ($10 \log 31.6 = 15$).

9-9 INTEGRATION

As the antenna scans a target, a train of pulses impinge on the target, as indicated in Sec. 3-9. For post-detection integration with a large number of pulses, the improvement factor is the square root of the number of pulses. That is, the numerator of the right-hand side of Eq. (3-14) is multiplied by $\sqrt{n}$, as follows:

$$R_{max} = \left[\frac{P_T A_e^2 \sigma \sqrt{n}}{4\pi\lambda^2 S_{min}L} \right]^{1/4} \tag{9-7}$$

A suitable scan rate, ω_s, is about 6 rpm or about 10 sec to make one revolution. If the antenna beamwidth is chosen to be $2°$, the beam will be on a target $\frac{2}{360}$ of a scan or $(2 \times 10)/360$ sec. With a repetition rate of 500, chosen in Sec. 9-6, the number of pulses impinging on the target in each scan is $\frac{20}{360} \times 500$ or almost 28. The square root of this is near enough to 5, and this value is used for $\sqrt{n}$ in the radar equation above.

9-10 PEAK POWER

Equation (9-7) is now used to determine the peak transmitted power, P_T, required. The target cross section σ is about 50 ft^2 for a military jet plane. Thus, substituting the values determined in the past few sections in Eq. (9-7),

$$135 \times 6080 = \left[\frac{P_T \times (16.5)^2 \times 50 \times 5}{4 \times 3.14 \times (0.328)^2 \times 1.2 \times 10^{-15} \times 31.6} \right]^{1/4}$$

Solving this expression for P_T yields a value about 350 000 watts. Using pulse compression with a compression ratio of 100, this could be reduced to 3.5 kw, which is a reasonable value for P_T. Actually, the decrease in power achievable by using chirp is not exactly a factor equal to the compression ratio, because in pulse compression the bandwidth is not $1/\tau$ but is instead $f_2 - f_1$. However, for this model, it may be assumed that a 5 kw peak power should take care of possible errors. The average power, from Eq. (1-2), is

$$P_A = P_p \times \tau f_r \qquad (9\text{-}8)$$

In this case, P_T is the peak power, and the average power is

$$P_A = 5000 \times 0.003 = 15 \text{ watts}$$

The effect of the antenna pattern's lobe structure, shown in Fig. 8-2, could increase the range if the target were at a beam maximum. Conceivably, also, a target may be completely undetectable if it is located at a pattern minimum. In general, the lobe structure tends to shift due to motions of the sea's surface, and of course the target is moving, so that the net effect is a further smoothing of the pattern, in addition to the effects mentioned in Sec. 8-4. Therefore, this effect is usually ignored in radar system calculations. However, it should be noted that the effect is observable, especially if the sea is calm.

9-11 ACCURACY OF DATA

If the echo signal is very strong compared to the receiver noise, the measurements of range, angle, and velocity can be made with confidence. However, when the signal-to-noise ratio at the receiver output is small, part of the problem of radar measurements is determining if, indeed, there is a signal present. There is a limit to the accuracy of all measurements, and, as might be expected, the accuracy of radar measurements decreases with lower signal-to-noise ratios. Since noise produces a randomly varying effect on the signals, measurement of parameters becomes a process of determining the statistical average values and determining the accuracy of these values.

9-12 RANGE ERROR

Since the output of the receiver is the sum of signal and noise, the effect of noise is to produce a random variation in the apparent amplitude of the echo. If the transmitted pulse were perfectly rectangular with zero rise time, the echo would also be perfectly rectangular. Amplitude variations due to noise would affect the shape of the pulse but not the rise time. Thus, there would be no variation in measurements of the time interval between the transmitted and received pulses. However, in practice it is impossible to achieve zero rise time. The noise then will also affect the received pulse during the rise time.

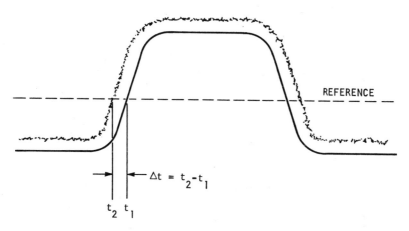

Fig. 9-2.   Range error.

Figure 9-2 indicates how noise affects the measurement of range. The *echo pulse* is the solid line in the figure. A reference amplitude or threshold is used to determine the time of arrival. The pulse in the figure crosses the reference amplitude at time t_1. If there were no noise, the operator would note that the range corresponds to the time interval $t_1 - t_0$, where t_0 is the time of transmission. However, noise added to the pulse makes the echo appear as the dotted line, which crosses the threshold earlier at t_2. Thus the target appears to be closer by a distance corresponding to $\Delta t = t_1 - t_2$. The value of Δt will be affected by the steepness of the leading edge of the pulse, that is, the rise time, and by the signal-to-noise ratio. The amount of error is given by

$$\Delta t = \frac{t_r}{(2S/N)^{1/2}} \tag{9-9}$$

where Δt is the error in time of arrival

   t_r is the rise time of the pulse

   S/N is the video rms signal-to-noise power ratio

From Eq. (9-9) it is evident that the error is directly proportional to the rise time and becomes smaller with stronger signals. It should be noted that this is a minimum error, and, in fact, it is usually larger.

9-13   ANGULAR ERROR

As the antenna beam sweeps past a stationary target, a train of pulses hits the target and echoes return to the receiver. The amplitudes of echoes will be strongest when the target is in the center of the beam and will fall off before and after this position is reached. Thus, the amplitudes of the pulses in the train are modulated, in effect, by the beam shape. If there were no noise to affect these amplitudes, it would be possible to determine the center of the train accurately. However, since the noise produces a random effect, some pulses on either side of the center may appear strongest, causing an erroneous measurement of angle of arrival.

The angular error is given approximately by

$$\sigma = \frac{\theta}{2\sqrt{(S/N)_0 n}} \tag{9-10}$$

where σ is the minimum error which can be achieved

θ is the half-power beamwidth of the antenna

$(S/N)_0$ is the rms signal-to-noise power ratio at the center of the train

n is the number of pulses hitting the target during the scan θ

(For signal-to-noise ratios less than one, the angular error will be much larger than σ given by Eq. 9-10.)

For example, assume an antenna half-power beamwidth of 4°. If the antenna scans through 360° in 9 sec, it scans through a beamwidth in 0.1 sec. If the pulse repetition rate is 1000, then 100 pulses will hit the target during the 4° scan. That is, $n = 100$. If the signal-to-noise ratio is 1.5 at the center of the beam, then

$$\sigma = \frac{4}{2\sqrt{1.5 \times 100}} = 0.16° \tag{9-11}$$

9-14 DOPPLER ERROR

The determination of the frequency of the returned echo is also affected by the noise. If in Fig. 9-2, the leading edge of the pulse is considered the rising portion of a sine wave, then the error Δt represents a phase error in the returned signal. The frequency error is similar in form to Eq. (9-9) and is given by

$$\Delta f = \frac{0.55}{\tau (2S/N)^{1/2}} \tag{9-12}$$

where Δf is the rms frequency error

τ is the pulse width

S/N is the video signal-to-noise power ratio

From Eq. (9-12) it is evident that the frequency error of the returned signal is inversely proportional to the pulse width and is less for stronger signals. The Doppler shift is the difference in frequency between the transmitted and received signals. Any error in frequency in the received signal is an error in the Doppler shift.

9-15 PULSE-COMPRESSION ERRORS

Noise also affects the accuracy of the frequency-modulated pulse-compression radar described in Sec. 7-7. The error in the time of arrival is

$$\Delta t_{pc} = \frac{0.55}{B(2S/N)^{1/2}} \tag{9-13}$$

where Δt_{pc} is the minimum error in time of arrival for a pulse-compression signal

B is the modulation bandwidth

S/N is the video signal-to-noise power ratio

Equation (9-13) is similar to Eq. (9-9) since a wide bandwidth implies a narrow pulse with a steep rise time.

The error in Doppler for a pulse-compression radar is

$$\Delta f_{pc} = \left(\frac{B}{4\tau S/N}\right)^{1/2} \tag{9-14}$$

where Δf_{pc} is the minimum frequency error for a pulse-compression signal

B is the modulation bandwidth

τ is the width of the FM pulse

S/N is the video signal-to-noise power ratio

The error in angle of arrival is no different for a pulse-compression radar. It is given by Eq. (9-10).

PROBLEMS

9-1. Which parameters listed in Sec. 9-2 affect transmitter design? Receiver design? Antenna design?

9-2. What is the maximum range at which an aircraft at an altitude of 2500 ft can be detected if the radar antenna is 100 ft above the sea surface? Compare this result to Eq. (9-1).   *ans:*   73.8 n.mi.

9-3. What antenna beamwidth is necessary to detect an aircraft at an altitude of 20 000 ft at a range of 12 n.mi.?   *ans:* 15°

9-4. Compute the five quantities of Table 9-1 for an *L*-band system operating at a frequency of 1000 MHz. Is the antenna size reasonable?

9-5. What is the gain of the *S*-band antenna of Table 9-1? The *C*-band antenna? Compare these values. What is the reason for this result? (Antenna gain is given by Eq. 9-2.)   *ans:* 34 db, 34 db

9-6. What is the ratio of attenuation caused by absorption at *X*-band to that at *S*-band?   *ans:* 11.1

9-7. The duty cycle of a radar display is defined as the time for the signal to be received from the maximum range divided by the time between transmitted pulses. What is the display duty cycle for the system of Sec. 9-6?   *ans:* 0.837

9-8. If the range resolution were changed from half a mile to 500 ft, what receiver sensitivity would be obtained in Sec. 9-7?   *ans:* −101 dbm

9-9. What scan rate would be required for the system discussed in the text if it were necessary for 50 pulses to hit the target?   *ans:* $3\frac{1}{3}$ rpm

9-10. At what range could a target with a 3 ft² cross section be detected with the system discussed in the text?   *ans:* 62.5 n.mi.

9-11. A particular radar transmits a rectangular pulse which is 10 μsec long (with a rise time of 5 μsec). What is the range resolution of this radar? With a signal-to-noise ratio of 17 db, what is the rms range error? The rms Doppler error?
                                    ans: 5000 ft, 250 ft, 5500 Hz

9-12. A certain pulse-compression radar uses a pulse width of 100 μsec and a bandwidth of 100 kHzO. What is the range resolution of this radar? If the signal-to-noise ratio is 17 db, what is the rms range error? The rms Doppler error? Compare the answers to those in Prob. 9-11.   *ans:* 5000 ft, 250 ft, 2800 Hz

CHAPTER TEN

Radar Testing

10-1 TYPES OF TESTS

Radar testing may be performed at three levels. At the first or lowest level, individual components and circuits are tested before installation to be certain they meet design specifications. They are then assembled into subassemblies and subsystems. Tests of these subsystems are the second category. The third is an overall test of the whole radar. In practice, the first class of tests is part of the design function. For example, an amplifier circuit may be designed to have a specific gain and bandwidth. After it is built, the gain and bandwidth are measured to be sure the circuit meets requirements. After assembly into a radar system, it is not likely to be tested again unless there is a failure. Thus, in troubleshooting, many first-level tests are repeated. However, these tests are not strictly radar tests, but radar servicing, and they will not be considered further here.

A radar has three major subsystems: the transmitter, the receiver, and the antenna. The second class of tests is evaluations of the performance of these subsystems. This second class and the third-class overall radar evaluation will be considered in this chapter. Since the method of evaluating the radar depends on the purpose of the radar, tests of search radars and tracking radars will be discussed separately.

10-2 TRANSMITTER TESTS

The parameters that must be measured in a transmitter are those which are used to evaluate system performance. These are the peak transmitted power P_T, the pulse width τ, and the pulse repetition frequency f_r. Peak power is rarely measured directly. Usually, the average power is measured by means of a calorimeter-wattmeter, and the peak power is calculated by dividing the average power by the duty cycle.

One form of calorimeter-wattmeter is a well-matched liquid load. The power is completely absorbed by the liquid. The fluid may be water, oil, or any liquid which is a good microwave absorber. The liquid flows through the load and is heated by the microwave energy. The temperature of the fluid is measured before and after it passes through the load. The average power can be calculated from the temperature difference, the time, and the known rate of flow. This type of calorimetric-wattmeter is usually supplied with a meter calibrated directly in power.

Ideally, the power should be measured at the antenna terminals by substituting the calorimeter-wattmeter for the antenna. This is usually impractical, and instead power is measured at the output of the transmitter. The attenuation between the transmitter and antenna may be ignored in the ideal case, but must be considered in the practical case.

The pulse width and repetition rate may be measured by an oscilloscope or even an indicator of the radar. The oscilloscope is synchronized with the pulse and the pulse width noted in centimeters or inches. The oscilloscope is calibrated by the insertion of an accurately calibrated marker (or using internal calibration) so that distance across the scope can be translated to time. Since the pulse is not perfectly rectangular, the width should be that of an equivalent rectangular pulse. For a trapezoidal pulse shape, this is the width at half the height; but for odd shapes, the equivalent width has to be evaluated by eye.

The repetition frequency is measured by a frequency counter which may also be included in the radar. It is, of course, the same as the synchronization frequency used to make the pulse width measurement.

10-3 RECEIVER TESTS

The important receiver parameters are the noise factor (or noise figure) and the bandwidth. Ideally, these should be measured at the antenna, just as in the case of the transmitter, but again it may be more convenient to make the measurements at the receiver input terminals. As before, in the latter case, the attenuation between the receiver and the antenna must be considered.

The bandwidth of the receiver is usually that of the IF amplifier. If this is known, the noise figure can be found easily by using the circuit of Fig. 10-1. With the signal generator disconnected, the output power meter reads only the noise in the receiver. Now the generator is connected and the output level is adjusted until the meter reads 3 db more than it did before. The signal power is the sensitivity of the receiver since it is 3 db more than the noise

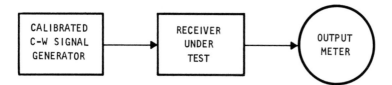

Fig. 10-1. Noise-figure measurement using signal generators.

power. Equation (7-2) can be used to calculate the noise figure. Solving
Eq. (7-2) for F_{db}:

$$F_{db} = S_{db} - 10 \log B + 171 \text{ dbm} \qquad (10\text{-}1)$$

A more reliable method of measuring noise figure utilizes a noise generator as illustrated in Fig. 10-2. At microwave frequencies, the noise generator
is a gas discharge tube in a suitable waveguide or coaxial line. The output of
the tube is constant across the frequency band and is accurately known. A
load is put at one end to absorb power going in the wrong direction. The
noise-figure meter at the output of the receiver under test has circuitry which
square-wave modulates the noise source. Then the noise output of the receiver with the noise source on is compared to the output with it off. The
noise figure is read directly on the meter. This method is faster and more
accurate than the signal generator method for low noise figures and does not
require a prior knowledge of bandwidth.

In measuring the noise figure of a superheterodyne receiver with a noise
source, it is important to know if the receiver has image rejection. With
image rejection, the noise figure is correct as measured and is termed the
single-channel noise figure. However, if there is no image rejection, twice as
much noise will pass through the IF amplifier. That is, the noise source puts
out all frequencies, and the frequencies above and below the l.o. frequency
which differ by the IF will go through. Thus, the noise figure read on the
meter, called the double-channel noise figure, will be 3 db less than the single-
channel value. To get the single-channel noise figure then, it is only necessary
to add 3 db to the reading. This problem doesn't arise when the noise figure
is measured with a signal generator.

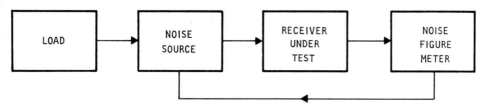

Fig. 10-2. Noise-figure measurement using noise source.

Ordinarily, it is unnecessary to make a bandwidth measurement, since the IF portion of the receiver is designed to have a specific bandwidth and usually has it when it is supplied. However, it is conceivable that the bandwidth might change with age, and measurements may be necessary when troubleshooting a faulty receiver. The measurement of bandwidth consists simply of checking output vs. frequency for a fixed input. This can be done point by point or by using a sweeper.

10-4 ANTENNA TESTS

The important antenna characteristics are the *gain* and the *pattern*. The pattern measurement reveals beamwidth and sidelobe levels. Ordinarily, when an antenna is supplied, these measurements have already been performed. However, it is sometimes necessary to check the antenna after it is installed.

The antenna pattern can be measured by the setup of Fig. 10-3. The antenna under test is rotated in azimuth or elevation as required and receives a signal from a distant transmitter and antenna from a varying angle. The distance between the two antennas must be large enough to permit the rays to be approximately parallel. An accepted value of the minimum distance is

$$R = \frac{2D^2}{\lambda} \qquad (10\text{-}2)$$

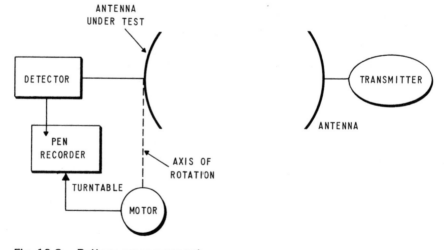

Fig. 10-3. Pattern measurement.

where R is the minimum range

   D is the diameter or width of the antenna

   λ is the free-space wavelength

During rotation, the detector output is fed to the pen of a recorder which is rotated synchronously with the antenna. A typical pattern was shown in Fig. 2-2. The 3-db beamwidth in this pattern is 20°. Major sidelobes are 14.5 db down and 15 db down, located at about 60° from the center of the main beam. Nulls occur about 30° on each side of the main beam, and there is no back lobe.

Gain measurements are made by comparing the received power using the antenna under test with that using a standard gain horn. Power from a remote antenna and transmitter is received by the radar antenna. A simple detector can be used with the radar antenna, or the radar receiver itself can be used. In either case, a reference level is noted. Now the standard gain horn, with gain higher than that of the antenna under test, is connected to the same detection system through a calibrated attenuator. The attenuation is adjusted so that the reading on the detector is identical with the first reading. The antenna gain is the gain of the standard horn less the attenuation necessary to reduce the signal to the reference level.

10-5 TESTING A SEARCH RADAR

The basic test of a search radar is a measurement of its ability to detect a target and determine the target's position. The best way to do this is to place a target of known size at a specified range and location and then to operate the radar in its normal mode of operation. The target may be a friendly plane flying a known path, or it may be a lightweight metal sphere dropped from a plane or carried aloft by a balloon. The sphere is preferable since it has a known cross section which does not change with aspect angle. The rate of fall of a dropping sphere is not easily controllable, but the rate of rise of a sphere connected to a balloon can be varied by changing the amount of inflation.

The signal produced in the receiver by the target echo can be checked against the theoretical echo predicted by the radar equation. This is done by setting the output of a calibrated signal generator to simulate the theoretical echo and by feeding this signal directly into the receiver. A comparison of the two yields a direct check on the radar's performance.

Sometimes it is necessary to check the overall performance of the radar system where it is impossible to obtain suitable target echoes. In this case an *echo box* is used. This is simply a resonant cavity with very high Q. It may be fixed-tuned to the radar frequency, or tunable if it is to be used with many radars or at many frequencies. In use, the transmitted signal is fed into the cavity (usually by a probe placed in front of the radar antenna), and the cavity is shock-excited so that it continues to "ring" after the transmitted pulse stops. The reradiated energy is an exponentially decaying signal which is picked up by the receiver until it is too weak to be detected. The time required for the signal to disappear from the receiver display is an indication of overall performance, since it is directly dependent on transmitter output, receiver sensitivity, and efficiency of the microwave plumbing.

10-6 TESTING A TRACKING RADAR

A tracking radar must not only be able to receive a target echo as predicted by the radar equation, but it must also be able to follow the target as it moves in three dimensions. Tests of a tracking radar, therefore, should determine if the radar satisfies both conditions. The compliance with the radar equation is checked by exactly the same method used with a search radar.

The ability of a tracking radar to track is derived from error signals produced when the antenna is not pointing directly at the target, as was explained in Sec. 6-3. One type of test to check this ability uses fixed targets at known ranges. The antenna is pointed away from the fixed target by a known amount, and the error signal is measured. In a dynamic test, the error signal is fed to the servos as it would be in operation, and the antenna is allowed to "seek" the target. When its motion stops, it is checked optically, using a transit or telescope.

The ability of the radar to track a moving target can be checked only by using a moving target. To track a point source, a small metal sphere is used as a target and is carried by a balloon. The true direction of the sphere is observed by accurate optical instruments. The pointing direction of the tracking radar is compared with the true direction.

When a tracking radar is following a plane instead of a point source, the strongest echo from the target may come from different parts of the plane as its aspect angle varies. As a result, the tracking radar may first follow one part of the plane and then jump to another. In an extreme case, the sudden change may cause the tracking radar to lose the target. To check the capability of the radar to track a scintillating target of this type, it should be tested against a plane flying a deliberately varying course. The larger the plane, the larger will be the scintillation, and consequently the more meaningful the test.

PROBLEMS

10-1. List the three major radar subsystems which are tested separately before the system is assembled.

10-2. What are the critical transmitter parameters? Describe how each can be measured.

10-3. The average output power of a radar with a 5-μsec pulse and p.r.f. of 100 pps is measured to be 20 watts. What is the peak output power of this transmitter?

ans: 40 kw

10-4. List the two major receiver parameters. Describe one way of measuring each parameter.

10-5. What is the difference between single-channel noise figure and double-channel noise figure?

10-6. The sensitivity of a receiver with a 1 MHz bandwidth is measured to be 10^{-13} watts. What is the noise figure of the receiver?   *ans:* 11 db

10-7. List four parameters which can be used to describe the antenna pattern. Describe how an antenna pattern is measured.

10-8. What is the minimum pattern measurement test distance for a 10 ft diameter antenna operating at X-band?   *ans:* 2000 ft

10-9. When measuring the gain of a certain antenna, it was found that the signal detected with a standard 30-db gain horn was 11 db stronger than the signal obtained with the antenna under test. What was the gain of the antenna under test?

ans: 19 db

10-10. What system properties are measured when testing search radars? Describe how these tests can be performed.

10-11. What is an echo box? How is it used in testing radar systems?

10-12. Describe how the error signals of a tracking radar can be tested. How is performance against moving targets determined?

10-13. How does target scintillation affect the operation of a tracking radar?

CHAPTER ELEVEN

Space Applications

11-1 RADAR ASTRONOMY

Radar astronomy is the study of celestial objects by means of radar. It differs from optical and radio astronomy in that the target is illuminated and the echo is received by the satellite-based or earth-based radar. In both optical and radio astronomy, the signals received are emissions from the observed objects or reflections by them of emissions from the sun or other sources in space.

The characteristics of radars used for radar astronomy can be specified from the requirements. They must detect targets at long ranges, and consequently the inter-pulse interval must be long. Thus, it takes almost two and a half seconds for a signal to get to our nearest celestial neighbor, the moon, and back. To send and receive a signal from the farthest known planet in our solar system would take 10 hr and to the nearest star about 7 yr.

There is little that a radar can learn about a celestial body that cannot be done better by optical means. However, the radar observations can verify and supplement optical observations. Radar does have one advantage in that it can be operated at anytime, i.e., when the sky is overcast and optical instruments are "grounded" or during the day when sunlight obscures observation of certain celestial bodies.

Radars have been built for observations of the moon. Since the round trip takes $2\frac{1}{2}$ sec, the repetition interval for these radars has been a minimum of 3 sec. Long pulses have been used to place as much energy as possible on the target. This permitted increasing receiver sensitivity by using narrow bandwidths. The observations did verify that the moon oscillated as it revolved, that the orbit around the earth was an ellipse (determined by Doppler shift), and that the surface of the moon was not smooth. However, the information is more accurately obtained by using optical instruments on lunar probes and man-made satellites.

Radar astronomy is a useful tool for determining the characteristics of the earth's atmosphere. Using the moon as a target, the location and ionization of layers can be determined by noting shifts in polarization of the moon echo.

It is unlikely that ground-based radars can be used effectively to learn the characteristics of planets and other objects beyond the moon. However, radars on man-made space vehicles can be used most effectively to probe the surfaces of planets with atmospheres impenetrable by optical instruments.

11-2 SATELLITE TRACKING

When man-made satellites are launched into known orbits, their positions at any moment can be predicted accurately. They can be observed and tracked optically on clear nights. Radar can be used advantageously to track them continuously whenever they are above the horizon, even during the day or when the sky is overcast. Since their orbits are known, radars can be programmed by computers to track the satellites without requiring the use of error signals. To simplify the tracking problem, most satellites carry beacons which emit signals stronger than could be achieved by radar echoes. These can be detected and tracked by *passive radars*, that is, radars which have only a receiver. Telemetry signals may be included to relay information (e.g., about weather) that the sensors on the satellite have observed.

11-3 SATELLITE DETECTION

Although it is the practice of the United States to announce all attempts to launch a satellite and of other world powers to announce all successful launchings, for political reasons it is necessary to have a capability to detect every satellite passing overhead. This capability does exist, and this, in fact, may be why nations do announce their launchings. It is impossible for a single radar to cover the entire sky searching for satellites. Instead, a network of radars is used, each patrolling a fixed portion of the sky.

It would be possible to cover an area as large as the United States with radars so that a satellite would always be in the beam of at least one radar. However, this is not economically feasible, nor is it necessary. Instead, a radar "fence" is created by using a line of radars so arranged that a satellite must pass through a radar beam to be over the United States. Information from this search-radar fence is then fed to tracking radars which quickly determine the satellite's orbit and future positions.

Tracking radars which can follow the satellite's progress are located in friendly countries around the world. The string of tracking radars forms a bracelet network with information on sightings and positions being passed from one station to the next as the satellite progresses.

11-4 DETECTION OF ICBM

The problem of detection of an ICBM launch by a hostile power is essentially the same as that of detecting a satellite. However, in order to be able to defend against it, it is necessary to acquire the missile at an earlier stage in its trajectory. Basically, it requires the same sort of radar fence, but located as near as possible to the suspected launch points. The problem is somewhat simplified in that, at any specific moment in history, a nation knows its potential enemies. Hence, the expected launch sites and directions of arrival are limited.

Index

Praise for Francis Ray's novels

BREAK EVERY RULE

"Classic Francis Ray...a joy to read."

—*Romance Reader*

"Francis Ray is a literary chanteuse, crooning the most sensual romantic fiction melodies in a compelling performance of skill and talent that culminates in another solid gold hit!" —*Romantic Times*

HEART OF THE FALCON

"A sizzler that will singe your mind with the laughter, tenderness, and passion that smolders between the pages." —*Romantic Times BOOKreviews*

ONLY HERS

"Ms. Ray continues to cut a swath across the lustrous fabric of romance history with *Only Hers*. Her inimitable style, irresistible humor, and extraordinary talent grace the pages of her books with the delicious

MORE...

tenacity of chocolate fudge swirls on French vanilla ice cream! She is one of the few authors who never disappoints her readers."

—*Romantic Times BOOKreviews*

ONE NIGHT WITH YOU

"Master craftswoman that she is, Francis Ray is gifted at creating heartwarming love scenes that never leave you hanging."   —*Romance in Color*

"Ruth Grayson is a force to be reckoned with as she sets her matchmaking sights on Faith's brother, since there is no such thing as happily single in Ruth's world. The steam the lovers create is a pleasure to behold. Ray never disappoints!"

—*Romantic Times BOOKreviews*

NOBODY BUT YOU

"A story that tugs at the heartstrings."

—*Romantic Times BOOKreviews*

"Not only does Francis Ray rock in this book but you also see a whole different side of racing that will keep you on the edge of your seat."   —*Night Owl Romance*

"A wonderful read."   —*Fresh Fiction*